STUDY GUIDE

52 WEEKS WITH JESUS

JAMES MERRITT

HARVEST HOUSE PUBLISHERS
EUGENE, OREGON

Cover by Dugan Design Group

Published in association with the literary agency of Wolgemuth & Associates, Inc.

52 WEEKS WITH JESUS STUDY GUIDE

Copyright © 2016 James Merritt
Published by Harvest House Publishers
Eugene, Oregon 97402
www.harvesthousepublishers.com

ISBN 978-0-7369-6554-5 (pbk.)
ISBN 978-0-7369-6555-2 (eBook)

Printed in the United States of America

22 23 24 / BP-GL / 10 9 8 7 6 5 4

52 Weeks with Jesus

This discussion guide has been prepared to help you get the most out of *52 Weeks with Jesus*, whether you are reading the book alone or as part of a group. Each chapter of this guide features three main sections.

In the first section, "Turn Your Eyes upon Jesus," you're invited to interact with some selected Bible passages that highlight the person, character, ministry, and teaching of Jesus Christ. Sometimes these passages will echo the texts featured in the corresponding chapter of the book; sometimes they will introduce new but related selections. In all cases, the texts and the discussion questions connected with them are designed to get you thinking about our amazing Savior.

The second section, "Reflect on the Book," directs you to three key quotations taken from each chapter of *52 Weeks with Jesus*. A series of discussion questions after each quotation encourages you to delve a little deeper into some of the main themes of the chapter.

The final section, "Put It into Practice," offers ideas to help you apply what you have learned. I want to encourage you to take the truth you have encountered and find ways to let it take root in your soul, so that you become increasingly like your Savior.

I pray that as you read the book and interact with this discussion guide, week by week you'll come to know, appreciate, and love the Lord Jesus more than you did the week before.

Just Like Us

Turn Your Eyes upon Jesus

1. Read Matthew 13:53-57.

   a. How did Jesus offend the people of his hometown? What in particular upset them?

   b. How does the "ordinariness" of Jesus still offend people? Why do you think God didn't make Jesus more like a Marvel comics character?

   c. In what ways was Jesus just like *you*? How does this make you feel? Explain.

2. Read Revelation 13:8.

   a. The "Lamb" mentioned in this verse is Jesus Christ (see Revelation 5:5-13). What does it mean that this Lamb was "slain from the creation of the world"? What does this say about God's plan for the world?

   b. Why would Jesus have a "book of life"?

   c. Compare this verse with Ephesians 2:10. What similarities in concept do you see between the two verses? How could these thoughts be important to you as you go about your daily life?

Reflect on the Book

1. "The next time your world seems to be spinning out of control and you wonder if someone has a hand on the throttle of the train, just read the first verse of the first chapter of the first book of the New Testament. You'll be

reminded that Jesus's tree is your tree and that God is in control."

   a. Describe a time your own world seemed to be spinning out of control.

   b. How does God intend for the genealogy of Jesus to encourage you during uncertain times? Does it? Explain.

2. "God can overcome whatever troubles are behind you to achieve the purpose he has set before you."

   a. What troubles behind you do you still need to overcome?

   b. What do you think God's purpose for you might be? Describe it.

3. "Jesus was just like us—born with a past and a history—and we have been made to become like him. God wants you to be a masterpiece of his grace by living for his glory and expressing his goodness to others."

   a. Why is it important that Jesus was "just like us," with a specific past and a history? Why is it important to you that Jesus was "just like us"?

   b. How can you live for God's "glory," right where you are? How can you express God's goodness to others? What can you do to help them see God through you?

Put It into Practice

1. Spend a little time investigating your own heritage. What does your genealogy tell you about who you are and where you come from?

2. Who in your sphere of influence most needs to see God's glory right now? What can you do this week to help this person see God's glory?

A Misfit Among Misfits

Turn Your Eyes upon Jesus

1. Read Isaiah 53:1-3.
   a. What does it mean that Jesus grew up like a "tender shoot" and like a "root out of dry ground" (v. 2 NIV)? At the time Jesus was born, what kind of status did Israel enjoy? What kind of status did the family line of David enjoy at that time?
   b. Would Jesus's physical features have attracted much attention (v. 2)? Would we probably have called Jesus handsome? Explain. Why do you think Isaiah would mention this detail?
   c. How would most men respond to Jesus, according to Isaiah's prophecy (v. 3)? In what way would Jesus be a "man of sorrows"? In what way would he be "familiar with suffering"? Why would men "hide their faces" from him? In what ways is Jesus still not "esteemed" today?
   d. Why do you think God gave Jesus the sort of body he had? Why not give him movie star looks and a throng of fans?

2. Read John 9:24-34.
   a. How did the religious leaders want the formerly blind man to "give glory to God" (v. 24)? What were they asking him to do? Why did they want him to do this?
   b. What one piece of testimony was the man willing to give (v. 25)?
   c. Why did the religious leaders begin to insult the man (vv. 26-28)?

d. What comparison did the leaders make between Moses and Jesus? What is significant about the comparison?

e. What conclusion did the man make on his own (vv. 30-33)?

f. What price did the man have to pay for choosing to speak the truth (v. 34)? Why do you think he was willing to pay it? Would you have been willing to pay it? Explain.

Reflect on the Book

1. "Jesus's genealogy in the Gospels includes five females. This sets the tone for justice and equality between the genders that is reinforced throughout Christ's ministry."

    a. How does the inclusion of five females in the genealogy of Jesus set "the tone for justice and equality"?

    b. How did the rest of Christ's ministry continue to set this tone?

2. "God seems to be saying that no one is beyond his grace—a message that Jesus reiterates repeatedly."

    a. Is it really true that no one is beyond God's grace? Explain. Describe someone in your own experience who appeared to be beyond God's grace, but wasn't.

    b. In what ways does Jesus reiterate that no one is beyond his grace? Does it ever feel to you as though *you* are beyond God's grace? Explain.

3. "God is reminding us that he can do for us what we cannot do for ourselves: pick up broken pieces and put them together, take broken lives and make them whole, gather broken hopes and make them reality."

    a. What broken pieces of your own life has God, through Christ, put back together?

    b. What hopes is God in the process of making reality for you?

Put It into Practice

1. Get alone somewhere and make a list of all the ways you feel like a "misfit." Then spend some time praying over that list, thanking God that he accepts you just as he accepts Jesus.

2. How has God been showing his grace in your life over the past week? Over the past month? Over the past year? Give him praise by telling someone else what you've watched him do in your life.

3

A Messy Messiah

Turn Your Eyes upon Jesus

1. Compare Isaiah 7:14 with Matthew 1:18-25 and Luke 1:26-38.

    a. How was Matthew careful to say that Mary was a virgin? Why was he so careful to say it?

    b. What language did Luke use to convey that Mary had not had sexual relations before she became pregnant? Why did he explain this was important to know?

    c. What would you say to someone who claimed the virgin birth couldn't be very important, since the apostle Paul never once mentioned it?

2. Read Ephesians 2:11-22.

    a. What was true of all non-Jews before the coming of Christ (vv. 11-12)?

    b. How did Christ change the Gentiles' ability to have a relationship with God? (v. 13) How did Christ make this change possible?

    c. In what way is Christ our "peace" (v. 14)?

    d. What did Jesus intend to create through his death on the cross (vv. 15-16)?

    e. How do we see the Trinity working together on our behalf (v. 18)? How does this truth affect you personally?

    f. How has your spiritual heritage changed because of what Christ did for you (vv. 19-22)? Name all the benefits you see.

Reflect on the Book

1. "The central point of Luke's genealogy is the fact that it *ends* in God."

    a. Why is it important that Luke's genealogy ends in God?

    b. In what way is it important to you that Luke's genealogy ends in God?

2. "Christ, the Son of God/ Became a son of Adam/ That we, sons of Adam,/ Might become sons of God."

    a. What does it mean that Jesus became a "son of Adam"? Why is it remarkable that "sons of Adam" could become "sons of God"?

    b. Why did Jesus have to become a son of Adam in order to make it possible for us to become sons of God?

3. "Just as God used two ordinary women named Ruth and Mary to make a lasting impact on the world, so God can use you to make a lasting impression on others by your living for him and loving him and doing his will."

    a. How do you think God might want to use you to make a lasting impression on others?

    b. In what ways is it especially hard for you to live for God? In what ways do you find it easy to love him? How might it be especially challenging to do his will this week? How will you meet that challenge?

Put It into Practice

1. What kind of Christian heritage do you want to leave to your family? What can you do, starting today, to begin leaving that kind of heritage?

2. Write a note to someone in your family (or to a friend), describing what he or she has done to encourage you to follow Jesus for the rest of your life.

4

Bread for the Journey

Turn Your Eyes upon Jesus

1. Compare Deuteronomy 8:3 with Matthew 4:1-4.

   a. How did God "humble" his people, according to Deuteronomy 8:3? Why did he do this? In what way is God's Word "bread"? Why is it necessary for life?

   b. Describe the temptation mentioned in Matthew 4. What was Satan trying to get Jesus to do? How did Jesus counter the temptation? How does his strategy provide us with an example for countering our own temptations?

2. Read John 6:25-59.

   a. Why did Jesus believe the people had gone looking for him? Did he rebuke them for this (vv. 25-26)? Explain. What instruction did he give them (v. 27)?

   b. How is believing "in the one [God] sent" the way to "do the works God requires"? How can "belief" be a "work" (vv. 28-29 NIV)?

   c. How did Jesus compare himself to manna (vv. 30-33)? What did he want to teach the people through this word picture?

   d. What claim did Jesus make in verse 35? What do you think he meant?

   e. How did the people respond to Jesus's claim in verse 41? Why did they respond in this way (v. 42)?

    f. What further comparisons did Jesus make between himself and manna (vv. 48-51)? How did the people respond to these comparisons (v. 52)?

    g. What claims did Jesus make in verses 53-58? What promises did he make? What do you think of these claims and promises? Why?

Reflect on the Book

1. "'What food is to your body I am to your soul,' Jesus said."

    a. How is Jesus like food for your soul?

    b. How do you, personally, "consume" the "food" of Jesus? How do you take him into your system?

2. "In one simple statement, Jesus reminds us that he is sustenance for all people in all places at all times."

    a. In what ways does Jesus sustain you?

    b. How has Jesus sustained you at various parts of your life? How have you been aware of his sustenance?

3. "There is a spiritual hunger in the human heart and an eternal hunger in the human soul that can never be satisfied with anything other than Jesus Christ, the Bread of Life."

    a. Describe what your own "spiritual hunger" felt like before you placed your faith in Christ.

    b. How is your "spiritual hunger" different now than it was before you placed your faith in Christ? How do you satisfy it?

Put It into Practice

1. Even if you're not used to the bread-making process, bake a loaf of bread from scratch. As you do so, think of all the ways Jesus wants to be the "bread of life" for you. Write down in a journal any new insights you have.

2. Make an appointment to observe some professional bakers at
   work. Note not only their culinary skills, but also the desires
   and needs of their customers. If it is appropriate at some
   point, see if you can initiate a casual conversation about
   Jesus, the Bread of Life.

5

Light in a Dark Place

Turn Your Eyes upon Jesus

1. Read John 1:4-9.
   a. How was Jesus's life the "light of men" (v. 4)?
   b. Why did not (and does not) the "darkness" understand the "light" (v. 5)?
   c. How did John testify to the light of Jesus (v. 8)?
   d. In what way is Jesus's light "true" (v. 9)? How does his light illuminate everyone?

2. Read John 8:12-20.
   a. What does Jesus mean that those who follow him will never walk in darkness (v. 12)? How are "light" and "life" connected in this passage?
   b. Where did Jesus come from? Where was he going (v. 14)?
   c. Why would someone know God the Father if they knew Jesus Christ (v. 19)?
   d. Why would the religious leaders have wanted to seize Jesus (v. 20)? Why didn't they do so?

Reflect on the Book

1. "Darkness runs for the hills when light comes. And Jesus is the light that banishes spiritual and emotional darkness."
   a. Describe a time when you witnessed darkness "running for the hills" when light came.
   b. What does spiritual and emotional darkness look like to you? How does Jesus banish it?

2. "Of the seven things that Jesus calls himself, this is the only title ["light"] that he also gives us. If you are a follower of Jesus Christ, you should also be light amidst the darkness."

   a. Why do you think Jesus calls his followers "light" but not "bread" or the "vine" or one of the other "I am" statements?

   b. How can you be light amidst the darkness in your neighborhood? At your work?

3. "Jesus called us to find people in dark places and to move toward those who need him."

   a. How can you find people in dark places? What dark places are especially accessible to you?

   b. Describe a specific way you can "move toward" someone you know who needs Jesus.

Put It into Practice

1. Get a concordance and look up all the times the Gospel of John uses the terms *light* and *darkness*. What do you discover about Jesus?

2. How does your local church strive to be the "light" that Jesus commissions it to be? How are you participating in these endeavors? If you are not currently involved in some kind of outreach, investigate what your church offers and determine to get involved. Determine when and how to make things happen.

6

An Open Door

Turn Your Eyes upon Jesus

1. Read Luke 13:22-30.

    a. What question prompted Jesus's answer in this passage (v. 23)?

    b. Why did Jesus speak of a "narrow door" (v. 24)? What kind of "effort" (NIV) does he have in mind? How many will unsuccessfully make an effort? Why is this significant?

    c. What story did Jesus tell to illustrate his main point (vv. 25-27)?

    d. What word picture did Jesus use to describe what's at stake (vv. 28-29)?

    e. What did he mean in verse 30? How does this summarize his teaching in this passage?

2. Read John 10:7-18.

    a. Who did Jesus call "thieves" and "robbers" (v. 8)? Why did he call them this?

    b. How does someone "enter" through the "gate" of Jesus (v. 9 NIV)? What can they expect to find when they enter?

    c. What comparison did Jesus make in verse 10?

    d. How did Jesus characterize himself in verse 11? What did he do?

    e. What comparison did Jesus make in verses 12-13?

f. What knowledge did Jesus claim to have in verse 14?

g. How is this knowledge like that of the Father (v. 15)?

h. Who are the "other sheep" mentioned in verse 16? (Remember that Jesus was speaking here to his Jewish countrymen.)

i. How many times did Jesus mention "laying down" his life in verses 7-18? Why is this significant?

Reflect on the Book

1. "The flock could rest only if the sheep knew that their shepherd was protecting them with his life."

   a. When do you find it hardest to rest securely? Why?

   b. How have you seen Jesus protect you in your walk of faith?

2. "Jesus put you here to live for him. He provides the purpose you've been pining for."

   a. How do you live for Jesus wherever he's put you? In what particular ways could you live for him more effectively?

   b. What is your purpose in life? Do you "pine" for something more? Explain.

3. "Are you secure in who you are, what you have, where you are going? Do you feel significant? Are you giving your life to things that matter and make a difference? Are you satisfied? Is there a settled peace in your heart when you go to bed and rise in the morning?"

   a. Answer the five questions above.

   b. Are you satisfied with the answers you just gave? Explain.

Put It into Practice

1. If you have not yet read the book *The Purpose Driven Life*,

get a copy and read it. Keep a journal to record your discoveries and insights. How can you start to live a more purposeful life?

2. Sit down sometime and write out an imaginary obituary for yourself. By the end of your life, what do you want to have accomplished? What would you want people to be able to truthfully say about you?

7

The Good Life

Turn Your Eyes upon Jesus

1. Read Isaiah 11:1-5.
   a. How does verse 1 picture the coming Messiah, Jesus? What is significant about these two pictures? What does it suggest about his earthly heritage?
   b. How does verse 2 picture the work and ministry of the coming Messiah? How does this line up with what you know of Jesus?
   c. What does it mean to "delight" in the fear of the Lord (v. 3)? Why would the Messiah *not* judge by what he heard or saw?
   d. What would be the Messiah's connection to the poor and needy (v. 4)?
   e. How does verse 5 characterize the coming Messiah? How does this compare with what you know of Jesus?

2. Read 1 Peter 5:1-5.
   a. What connection did Peter make between suffering and glory (v. 1)? Why is this significant?
   b. What metaphor did Peter use to describe spiritual leaders in the church (v. 2)? How are they to discharge their duties?
   c. What contrast did Peter make in verse 3?
   d. Why did Peter mention "the chief Shepherd" (v. 4)? What is the connection between the "glory" mentioned in verse 4 and that mentioned in verse 1?

    e. What is a primary characteristic God expects from all followers of Christ, but especially of leaders (v. 5)? Why does he expect this?

Reflect on the Book

1. "That's the position Satan will always take in your life. Driving you, shoving you from the rear with reminders of your past, filling you with guilt and anxiety, riddling you with fear and uncertainties in the present, whispering to you worries about the future."

    a. Describe a time in your life when you believe Satan was driving you from the rear.

    b. In what areas of your life is Satan most likely trying to drive you? How can you give these areas over to the leading of the Shepherd?

2. "Jesus does not guard us *from* difficulty; he guards us *in* difficulty."

    a. Why do you think Jesus tends to guard us *in* difficulty rather than guarding us *from* difficulty? What is his goal?

    b. How is Jesus currently guarding you in difficulty?

3. "Two things make a shepherd *good*. He always leads the sheep where they need to go, and he always gives the sheep what they need to have."

    a. Where does Jesus appear to be leading you right now? Where is it that you need to go?

    b. What things do you currently lack that you think you need to have? Why do you think your Shepherd has not (at least not yet) given them to you?

Put It into Practice

1. Visit a farm or a county fair or state fair and strike up a conversation with someone who raises sheep. Find out

as much as you can about what it takes to care for these animals.

2. When you are gathered in a small group study, quiz every member about how he or she tries to discern the leading of the Good Shepherd. Have someone write down all the insights, and then as a group, take the best insights and develop a "guide" on following the lead of Christ.

8

A Grave Buster

Turn Your Eyes upon Jesus

1. Read Psalm 13.

   a. What was the primary struggle of the writer in this psalm (v. 1)? Have you ever felt like this? If so, when and why?

   b. What struggle did the psalmist have in the first half of verse 2? What was his struggle in the second half of the verse?

   c. What plea did the psalmist make in verse 3?

   d. Despite the psalmist's anguish, what statement did he make (v. 5)? In what does he "rejoice"?

   e. Why did the psalmist expect to "sing" (v. 6)?

   f. In what way does this psalm often mirror the experience of followers of Jesus?

2. Read 1 Corinthians 15:50-58.

   a. What can't "flesh and blood" inherit (v. 50)? Why not?

   b. What event is depicted in verses 51-52? What was important to Paul about this event?

   c. What did Paul expect to get "swallowed up" in victory (v. 54)?

   d. What kind of song did this thought cause Paul to sing (v. 55)? Why?

   e. From where does the Christian's victory come (v. 57)?

   f. How should this knowledge affect the way we live (v. 58)?

Reflect on the Book

1. "Jesus took time to assure us that, no matter how long you wait, he is never late."

   a. In what area of life do you currently need a reminder that Jesus is never late? Explain.

   b. Name some good thing for which you've been waiting a long time. What good has come of your waiting so far?

2. "If you are a believer in Jesus Christ, your life is not going to end in death…it will *lead* to death, but because you have eternal life, it *ends* in the glory of God."

   a. If you were to die today, how would your life have glorified God?

   b. How can you be sure you have eternal life? How will your life eternally give glory to God?

3. "Whatever Jesus is doing in your life, he's doing not primarily to satisfy you but to glorify God."

   a. In what area of your life do you feel most dissatisfied? How can that area of your life still glorify God?

   b. Why is God so concerned that your life should give glory to him? Why is his glory so important?

Put It into Practice

1. Keep a journal for at least a month, recording all those times when it feels to you as though Jesus is "late" in coming to your aid. Write down your feelings. But also be sure to go back to the journal and record when Jesus decisively acts. What do you learn from this exercise?

2. Get a concordance and do a study of the biblical phrase "wait on the Lord." What do you discover?

9

A One-Way Street

Turn Your Eyes upon Jesus

1. Read Isaiah 45:18-23.

    a. Why did God say he created the world (v. 18)?

    b. How does God *not* speak, according to verse 19? What does he *not* say? If he does not say these things or speak in this way, what and how does he speak?

    c. What instruction did God give in verse 20? To whom did he give it? How did he describe those who seek gods other than himself?

    d. What evidence did God give for his claims to exclusive deity (v. 21)? How did he describe himself?

    e. What plea did God make in verse 22? To whom did he make this plea?

    f. What promise did he make in verse 23? Compare this with Philippians 2:9-11.

2. Read John 14:1-14.

    a. Why should the hearts of Jesus's followers be untroubled (v. 1)?

    b. What truth did Jesus give in verse 2?

    c. What promise did Jesus make in verse 3?

    d. Why did Jesus believe his disciples knew "the way" to the place he was going (v. 4)?

    e. What exclusive claim did Jesus make in verse 6?

    f. Once someone has seen Jesus, why do they know what the Father is like (v. 9)?

g. What is the relationship between Jesus and the Father (vv. 10-11)?

h. What is the relationship between Jesus and his followers (vv. 12-14)?

Reflect on the Book

1. "If any religion works as well as the next, Good Friday becomes *Dumb* Friday. Why would a loving God allow his Son to experience a brutal execution if it wasn't necessary?"

   a. Do you think God the Father saw Jesus's execution as "good"? Explain.

   b. What was the purpose for Jesus's execution having to be "brutal"? Why couldn't he have had a less violent death?

2. "Jesus tells us that the highway to God is a *freeway*. No toll is required to get on it, and this freeway has already been built and paid for."

   a. Explain how the highway to God is a "freeway." Who built and paid for this freeway?

   b. Are you traveling on this freeway? Explain. When and how did you get on it?

3. John 14:6 "sets Jesus apart from every other spiritual figure who ever lived. He didn't just say, 'Come to me, and I'll show you the way.' Jesus said, 'I *am* the way.'"

   a. Why did Jesus say he was *the* way to God?

   b. Why is Jesus different from every other spiritual figure who ever lived? How would you respond to someone who said Jesus was just one religious leader among many?

Put It into Practice

1. Do a quick research project by asking a dozen strangers or passersby how people can draw close to God. What seems to be the common belief in your area?

2. Write out a defense of why Jesus would say he is *the* way to God. Use as many corollary Scripture passages as you think are relevant. What kind of a case can you build?

The Root of the Fruit

Turn Your Eyes upon Jesus

1. Read John 15:1-11.

   a. In what way is Jesus the "true" vine (v. 1)? In what way is his Father the "gardener" (NIV)?

   b. Why does the Father prune the branches (v. 2)?

   c. What does Jesus's "word" do for his followers (v. 3)?

   d. What is the only way that Jesus's followers can produce spiritual fruit (v. 4)?

   e. What can Jesus's followers accomplish if they do not remain "in" him (v. 5)?

   f. To what did Jesus compare followers who do not remain "in" him (v. 6)?

   g. What promise did Jesus give in verse 7?

   h. How can Jesus's followers identify themselves as his disciples (v. 8)? How does the Father respond to this?

   i. What is the relationship between love for Jesus and obeying his commands (vv. 9-10)?

   j. What kind of joy does Jesus want us to have (v. 11)? How do we experience this joy?

2. Read Galatians 5:16-19.

   a. How can we avoid engaging in the kind of activity that displeases God (v. 16)? How does one do this, practically speaking?

   b. What is the core of our problem (vv. 17-18)?

c. How do we overcome the problem (v. 19)? What does this look like in real life?

Reflect on the Book

1. "For what purpose has God put people on this planet? Jesus says, *to bear fruit.*"

   a. What are some practical ways that Jesus's followers can and should "bear fruit"?

   b. How are you "bearing fruit"? Are you satisfied with your production? Explain.

2. "If you want to bear the fruit of Christ, you have to connect with and concentrate on Christ."

   a. How do you most effectively connect with Christ?

   b. Describe a couple of ways that you like to concentrate on Christ.

3. "The hand of the gardener is never closer to the branch than when he is pruning."

   a. If God loves us, why does he subject us to the painful process of pruning?

   b. In what ways is God pruning you right now? What kind of help could you use from others, if any, to better profit from the experience?

Put It into Practice

1. Do a short Internet study on fruit trees. What does it take to grow healthy fruit? What parallels can you see between this kind of farming and spiritual growth?

2. If you have some plants that need pruning, get some shears and go to work. As you work, meditate on how God prunes you to make you increasingly resemble his Son.

11

A Man of Marvels

Turn Your Eyes upon Jesus

1. Read Isaiah 35:1-6.

   a. How do verses 1-2 picture the coming of the Messiah? How does this picture compare with the coming of Jesus?

   b. How do verses 3-4 picture the ministry of Jesus?

   c. How does the activity of verse 5 set apart the Messiah? (Hint: no Old Testament prophet ever healed a blind man.) How does this verse characterize the ministry of Jesus?

   d. How does verse 6 also illustrate the ministry of Jesus? What two pictures are presented here? How were each fulfilled in Jesus's ministry?

2. Read Luke 4:14-21.

   a. What does it mean that Jesus returned to Galilee "in the power of the Spirit" (v. 14)?

   b. What personal custom of Jesus is mentioned in verse 16? Why is this significant?

   c. Why do you think Jesus chose to read aloud Isaiah 61:1-2 in Luke 4:18-19?

   d. What kind of ministry did Isaiah depict? Why would Jesus focus on this description?

   e. In what way was the text of Isaiah "fulfilled" by Jesus in the hearing of the people in the synagogue at Nazareth (v. 21)?

Reflect on the Book

1. "Jesus performed miracles to authenticate what he said and who he was: God's only Son."

   a. What miracles of Jesus speak loudest to you about who he is? Explain.

   b. What would you say to someone who said he doubted Jesus ever performed any miracles at all?

2. "The ultimate purpose of everything that Jesus said and did was to glorify his Father."

   a. Why was Jesus so committed to glorifying his Father?

   b. How did Jesus's life bring ultimate glory to the Father? How can your life better mimic his?

3. "The message always trumps the miracle."

   a. Why does the message always trump the miracle? What does this mean?

   b. Imagine you lived during the time described in 2 Thessalonians 2:9-10. How would you respond to these kinds of miracles?

Put It into Practice

1. Watch a good magician or illusionist perform. How does what he or she does differ from what Jesus did?

2. Investigate the kind of spiritual deception that will take place in the period just before Jesus returns (see, for example, Matthew 24:4-5,11,24). How can what you learn about that time help you to become more discerning right now?

Crisis Manager

Turn Your Eyes upon Jesus

1. Compare Deuteronomy 10:12-16 with 1 Corinthians 7:35.

   a. What five things did God ask his people to do in Deuteronomy 10:12-13? What did he say would be the result of doing these things (v. 13)?

   b. What does God own, according to verse 14?

   c. Given verse 14, why is verse 15 especially surprising?

   d. What does it mean to "circumcise" one's heart (v. 16)? What does it mean to be "stiff-necked" (NIV)?

   e. Although Paul's instruction in 1 Corinthians 7:35 is about something very different, both passages share two primary concerns. What are they? How do these concerns relate to *all* of life?

2. Read Matthew 7:21-23 and Luke 6:46-49.

   a. What warning did Jesus give in Matthew 7:21?

   b. What will "many" people say to Jesus on the day of judgment (v. 22)? How will Jesus reply to them (v. 23)?

   c. What question did Jesus ask in Luke 6:46? What response do you think he expected to hear?

   d. What illustration did Jesus use to describe those who obey his commands (vv. 47-48)? What illustration does Jesus use to describe those who ignore his words (v. 49)?

   e. What common thought do these two passages from Matthew and Luke both develop? What point does Jesus want us to understand?

Reflect on the Book

1. "Our problems are Jesus's possibilities."

    a. What keeps this statement from being more than just a motivational cliché?

    b. What problems are you facing right now that Jesus can use to create new possibilities for you?

2. "What matters to us matters to Jesus."

    a. When are you most likely to wonder whether what matters to you *really* matters to Jesus?

    b. Do the things that matter to Jesus also matter to you? Explain.

3. "Jesus never met a problem that he could not solve if the afflicted only do what he tells them to. Too many of us know what Jesus wants us to do, but refuse to do it."

    a. What do you believe Jesus is telling you to do right now regarding a particular challenge or difficulty in your life?

    b. Why do we resist doing what Jesus wants us to do?

Put It into Practice

1. Make a list of the ten biggest problems you are currently facing. Commit these things to prayer over the next several weeks. Write down how Jesus interacts with you over these difficulties. Make sure to praise him for the answered prayer you receive.

2. Do a word study in the New Testament of the terms *obey* and *obedience*. What do you discover?

Captain of My Ship

Turn Your Eyes upon Jesus

1. Read Isaiah 43:1-7.
    a. How did God describe himself in verse 1? What instruction did he give in verse 1?
    b. What promises did God give in verse 2?
    c. How did God describe himself in verse 3? How was this intended to intensify the promise?
    d. How did God describe his people in verse 4? How much were they worth to him?
    e. What did God promise to do in verses 5-6?
    f. For what ultimate purpose did God make his people (v. 7)?

2. Read Mark 4:35-40.
    a. What did Jesus command his disciples to do in verse 35?
    b. Who witnessed what was about to take place (v. 36)?
    c. What happened in transit (v. 37)?
    d. What was Jesus doing during this time (v. 38)? How did his disciples react?
    e. How did Jesus respond to the disciples' actions (v. 39)? What happened?
    f. What two questions did Jesus ask his disciples (v. 40)? In what way does he still ask these two questions to us?

Reflect on the Book

1. "The sun may quit shining, the wind may start blowing, and

the waves may begin crashing, but Jesus never fails to keep his promises."

   a. What promises of Jesus are most precious to you? Why?

   b. Describe a time when a fierce storm hit, and you experienced Jesus keeping a promise in the middle of that trial.

2. "Even if you live as holy a life as is possible and fall deeply in love with Jesus, you will still face storms. Many times these squalls come when we are closest to Jesus."

   a. Why do you think God allows storms to trouble the lives of those who love him?

   b. What have you learned about God when you've suffered through a storm? What have you learned about yourself?

3. "It may sound shocking, but *we need storms*. Christ allows us to sail into them so we'll remember his promises, rest in his presence, and rely on his power."

   a. Describe a time when you saw clearly that *you* needed to go through a storm.

   b. What are some practical ways to rest in Jesus's presence during a storm? How do you rely on his power rather than trying to depend on your own?

Put It into Practice

1. The next time you are in a storm of the weather kind, use it as an opportunity to pray. Ask God to show you how to better weather the many other kinds of storms that hit you and your household.

2. Interview someone in your church whom you know has weathered some terrible storm. Ask him or her to tell their story, and listen for wisdom that you can use in your own life.

A Miraculous Multiplier

Turn Your Eyes upon Jesus

1. Read Exodus 4:1-9.

   a. When God commissioned Moses to lead his people out of Egyptian slavery, Moses had a key question. What was it (v. 1)?

   b. To what did God direct Moses's attention (v. 2)?

   c. What did God instruct Moses to do with the object (v. 3)? What happened when Moses complied?

   d. What did God instruct Moses to do next (v. 4)? What happened?

   e. What reason did God give Moses for the events that had just transpired (v. 5)? How were events like these supposed to authenticate Moses's commission and message?

   f. What further corroborating pieces of evidence did God give to Moses (vv. 6-9)? Why do you think God gave Moses multiple options?

2. Read John 6:1-15.

   a. Who followed Jesus (vv. 1-2)? Why did they follow him?

   b. What was the setting for this incident (vv. 3-4)? Is anything significant about it?

   c. What did Jesus ask Philip (vv. 5-6)? Why did he ask this question?

   d. How did Philip respond to Jesus's question (v. 7)?

e. How did Andrew respond (vv. 8-9)? What question did he ask?

f. What did Jesus instruct his disciples to do (vv. 10-11)? What did he himself do?

g. What happened next (vv. 12-13)?

h. How did the crowd respond to what happened (v. 14)?

i. How did Jesus respond to what the crowd intended to do (v. 15)?

Reflect on the Book

1. "When Jesus asks you for anything, trust that it isn't just a request but a test."

   a. When was the last time you thought Jesus had tested you? What happened?

   b. How do you normally respond to Jesus's tests? How could you respond better?

2. "God has a habit of using little things to accomplish unbelievable things."

   a. Describe a time in your life when God used a little thing to accomplish something big.

   b. What "little things" in your life right now might be candidates for God to use for something incredible?

3. "Jesus always blesses what he uses."

   a. How would you define Jesus's "blessing"?

   b. How might Jesus want to use *you* to bless someone else?

Put It into Practice

1. Get alone by yourself and think through the last five years of

your life, looking for those times when you believe God put you through a test. What happened in each case?

2. Determine to be a "secret blessing" to someone in your neighborhood who really needs it. Write them an encouraging, anonymous card, secretly drop off some goodie you know they like, or do something else equally welcome. And don't give away your secret!

A Leader Worth Following

Turn Your Eyes upon Jesus

1. Read 2 Samuel 7:8-10.

   a. What title did God use to describe David in verse 8? How did God remind David of his history? Why did he do this? What contrast did he make?

   b. How did God further remind David of his history in verse 9? How did he use that history as a foundation for making a promise? Describe the promise.

   c. To whom does the focus shift in verse 10? What promises did God make there? What do those promises have to do with David?

2. Read Luke 2:51; John 6:38; Luke 4:1.

   a. How did the boy Jesus respond in Luke 2:51 to his mother's expression of concern in Luke 2:48? What does this tell you about his relationship to authority?

   b. What was Jesus's "mission statement," according to John 6:38? What does this tell you about his adult relationship to authority?

   c. Where did Jesus go, according to Luke 4:1? Why did he go there? Did he choose to go there without reference to anyone else's desire? What does this tell you about his relationship to authority even at the beginning of his ministry?

Reflect on the Book

1. "A key principle of Jesus's leadership philosophy [is that] the way to lead is to learn how to follow."

   a. Who are some of the best leaders you know personally? What makes them such good leaders?

   b. How did the leaders you just described first learn to follow? How did they learn to be good leaders?

2. "The first lesson Jesus wants you to learn is not how to be over but how to be under."

   a. What is the hardest thing about learning how to be "under"? What do you most struggle with personally?

   b. Think of the worst leader you know. Does he or she most struggle with being "over" or "under"? Explain.

3. "When you learn how to recognize and respect leadership, when you know how to follow, you'll learn how to lead."

   a. How do you "respect leadership"? Do your leaders know that you respect them? Explain.

   b. Is it possible to be both a leader and a follower in the same group? Explain.

Put It into Practice

1. Show how much you respect a leader at church by doing something unexpectedly kind or helpful for the person. Let the individual know how much you appreciate his or her efforts on your behalf.

2. Identify the best follower you know, and ask the person for his or her "secret." The person probably won't know what to say, but gently prod. What can you learn?

The Great Empathizer

Turn Your Eyes upon Jesus

1. Read Luke 10:17-20.

   a. What excited the group of seventy-two disciples whom Jesus had sent out to minister (v. 17)?

   b. How did Jesus describe their ministry (vv. 18-19)?

   c. What did Jesus consider a bigger cause for celebration (v. 20)? Why?

2. Read Mark 2:1-12.

   a. What happened when Jesus returned home (vv. 1-2)?

   b. Who also came to see Jesus (v. 3)?

   c. What problem did these men have to overcome (v. 4)? How did they overcome it?

   d. What did Jesus see (v. 5)? What did he say in response?

   e. How did some religious leaders react to this incident (vv. 6-7)?

   f. How did Jesus react to the religious leaders (vv. 8-9)? What question did he ask them? How would you have answered the question?

   g. What miracle did Jesus perform in response to the faith of the friends of the disabled man (vv. 10-11)?

   h. How did this story end (v. 12)? What effect did the incident have on the crowd?

Reflect on the Book

1. "Jesus gets excited when he sees our faith."

   a. Why do you think Jesus gets excited when he sees our faith? What's exciting about it?

   b. When was the last time you think Jesus got excited to see *your* faith? Explain.

2. "Christianity is the only spiritual philosophy that addresses our greatest problem, which is sin, and meets our greatest need, which is forgiveness."

   a. Why is our greatest problem sin?

   b. Does forgiveness eliminate sin? Explain.

3. "When I can stand before a holy and righteous God and declare that because of the cross my sins are forgiven, Jesus gets excited."

   a. Will you be able to stand before God and declare that your sins are forgiven? Explain.

   b. How does forgiveness of sin affect the way you behave now?

Put It into Practice

1. Do something this week that can't help but stretch your faith. If you just can't get yourself to do this alone, try some new venture with someone else.

2. If you have had a hard time forgiving someone, read the book *Forgive to Live* by Dick Tibbits. Look for specific strategies that will help you to forgive, and then put them into practice.

The Divine Ophthalmologist

Turn Your Eyes upon Jesus

1. Read Matthew 9:27-30; 12:22; 15:30-31; 20:29-34; 21:14.

    a. Summarize the story in Matthew 9:27-30. Who wanted Jesus's attention? Why? How did Jesus heal them?

    b. What was the problem in Matthew 12:22? Who needed Jesus's attention? What did Jesus do, and what was the result?

    c. What are the needs mentioned in Matthew 15:30-31? How did the crowd respond to Jesus's healings?

    d. Who wanted Jesus's attention in Matthew 20:29-34? Why? How did Jesus heal them?

    e. Where did the scene described in Matthew 21:14 take place? What happened?

2. Read Philippians 2:12-16.

    a. What commands and instructions were given in verse 14?

    b. What reason was given for complying with these instructions (v. 15)? What word pictures were used to describe those who comply?

    c. What did Paul assume these believers were doing as they went about their regular lives (v. 16)? How did their behavior reflect on his ministry?

    d. How does God want people in this world to "see" an unseen God?

Reflect on the Book

1. "Augustine [once said], 'I cannot show you my God—not because there is no God to show you, but because you have no eyes to see him.'"

    a. What does it mean to have eyes to see God? Why can't some people see God?

    b. Do you have eyes to see God? Explain.

2. "A place of desperation is a setting for God's transformation."

    a. Why is a place of desperation often a setting for God's transformation?

    b. What places of desperation have been settings for God's transformation in your own life?

3. "Because this man had responded to the *first* light that Jesus had offered him, he now received the *full* light of who Jesus was."

    a. What new thing are you learning about Jesus through this study? How are you responding to that new insight?

    b. Think of a person you know who seems to know Jesus deeply. What about that person makes you think this? Would you like to be more like him or her? Explain.

Put It into Practice

1. Listen to an interview with a currently famous atheist. Look for clues to understand why that person can't seem to see God. What do you learn?

2. Read the bestseller *Unbroken*, about the life of Louis Zamperini. How did some awful places of desperation set him on a path to amazing transformation?

Spiritually Sovereign

Turn Your Eyes upon Jesus

1. Read Mark 5:1-20.

    a. Who came out to meet Jesus (vv. 1-5)? How did Mark describe the man? What was his problem?

    b. How did the man respond to Jesus (vv. 6-7)?

    c. What prompted this man to act in this way (v. 8)?

    d. What was the man's core problem (v. 9)?

    e. How did Jesus respond to the man's need (vv. 10-13)? What happened?

    f. How did people from the area respond to what had taken place (vv. 14-17)? Why did they respond in this way?

    g. What did the man want to do after his healing (v. 18)?

    h. What did Jesus instruct the man to do instead (v. 19)?

    i. What happened as a result of the whole incident (v. 20)?

2. Read Acts 5:15-16; 8:5-8; 19:11-12.

    a. Why did people gather around Peter in Jerusalem (Acts 5:15-16)? What did they hope to receive? What happened? What was the significance of these events?

    b. Why did people gather around Philip in Samaria (Acts 8:5-8)? What did they hope to receive? What happened? What was the significance of these events?

    c. Why did people gather around Paul in Ephesus (Acts

19:11-12)? What do you think they hoped to receive? What happened? What was the significance of these events?

Reflect on the Book

1. "Satan and his demons are in the life-taking business; Jesus is in the life-giving business."

   a. How do Satan and his demons most often take "life" away from people? Where do you see this taking place now?

   b. What does it look like when Jesus gives life to someone? What are the outward signs?

2. "Demons do have great power. But demons are no match for Jesus or for any follower of Christ in whom Jesus lives."

   a. Why are demons no match for Jesus? Why are they no match for a dedicated follower of Jesus?

   b. Who in your web of relationships really needs to see the power of Jesus? How might you be a conduit of his power?

3. "When you trust Christ as your Savior and God's Spirit comes to live within you, demons will attack you, but they can never possess or defeat you."

   a. Describe a demonic attack you believe you have suffered. What happened?

   b. Why can demons never possess or defeat a genuine follower of Christ? How does this give you encouragement and hope?

Put It into Practice

1. Why do you think stories of encounters between demonic forces and faithful believers in Jesus are more common

outside of the Western world? Do some research to find out more about these encounters.

2. Offer to volunteer at a local city mission. After your time of volunteering, ask a leader to tell you some stories of how Jesus has broken through the spiritual darkness of people who have come to the mission.

The Seed Sower

Turn Your Eyes upon Jesus

1. Read Matthew 13:1-23.

   a. Why do you think Jesus taught about evangelism using a parable?

   b. What happened to the seed in verse 4? On what kind of soil did it land? Is this seed any different from the other seed? Explain.

   c. What happened to the seed in verses 5-6? On what kind of soil did it land?

   d. What happened to the seed in verse 7? On what kind of soil did it land?

   e. What happened to the seed in verse 8? On what kind of soil did it land? What was the result? What do you think caused the difference in yield?

   f. Why would Jesus speak the advisory in verse 9 at this point in the parable?

   g. What question did the disciples ask Jesus in verse 10? What do you think prompted the question?

   h. How did Jesus reply in verses 11-17? How would you summarize his essential answer?

   i. How does verse 4 relate to verse 19?

   j. How do verses 5-6 relate to verses 20-21?

   k. How does verse 7 relate to verse 22?

   l. How does verse 8 relate to verse 23?

2. Read 1 Corinthians 3:5-9.

   a. How did Paul characterize himself and Apollos (v. 5)?

   b. What various functions were described in verse 6? Why is each important?

   c. Who had the key task (v. 7)? Why?

   d. How did Paul see the tasks of evangelism (v. 8)? What did he see as one result for the evangelist?

   e. What three descriptions did the apostle offer in verse 9? In what way is each one important? What does each convey?

Reflect on the Book

1. "Evangelism is not dependent on the sower or the seed but on the soil. It is the receptivity of the person that determines whether or not our evangelistic efforts succeed or fail."

   a. Do you consider yourself gifted in evangelism? Explain.

   b. Think of five people you know who need Jesus. What kind of "soil" do you think each possesses?

2. "A seed cannot plant itself. It needs a sower."

   a. What would it take for you to become a more effective sower?

   b. When was the last time you spoke with a non-Christian about Jesus? Describe the encounter.

3. "Jesus only asks you to share what you know and live what you share."

   a. Consider your experience with Jesus in the past year. Which of your experiences might be especially helpful to someone who doesn't yet know Jesus?

   b. Would your acquaintances be surprised to hear you're a Christian? Explain.

Put It into Practice

1. Compile a list of five people you know who need to place their faith in Jesus. Commit to pray for them regularly for at least several months.

2. Write out a short version of your testimony. How did you come to faith in Jesus? What has happened since you came to faith? What is Jesus doing in your life now?

20

The Best Boss

Turn Your Eyes upon Jesus

1. Read Matthew 20:1-16.

   a. Describe the basic setup of this story (vv. 1-2).

   b. What new wrinkle occurs in verses 3-4? What are the terms of employment offered?

   c. What additional wrinkles occur in verse 5? What terms of employment are offered?

   d. What additional wrinkle occurs in verses 6-7? What, if anything, is different this time around?

   e. How did Jesus conclude his story in verses 8-12? What is important about the last workers hired being paid first?

   f. How does the owner in the story respond to workers' objections (vv. 13-15)? What do you think of his logic?

   g. How did Jesus summarize his teaching (v. 16)?

2. Read Colossians 3:22–4:1.

   a. What general instructions did Paul give slaves in verse 22? What is the overarching concern of this instruction?

   b. What instructions did Paul give in verses 23-24? How are these instructions applicable to the entire Christian life?

   c. What warning was given in verse 25?

   d. How does the instruction to masters correspond to the instruction to slaves (4:1)? What reminder is given to support this instruction?

Reflect on the Book

1. "Grace puts us in our place."

   a. In what way does grace put us in our place? What does this phrase mean?

   b. How do you see Jesus dealing with you in grace? Where do you most see this?

2. "God doesn't have to invite anybody to be a part of his family, to be a citizen in his kingdom, or to be a worker in his ministry… his only motivation is grace."

   a. Why doesn't God owe anyone anything?

   b. How do you reflect God's grace to others? How do you pass it along?

3. "Look at everything you have. Not just materially but relationally, socially, financially, and even physically and realize that *it is all just grace.*"

   a. Is there any such thing as a "self-made man" (or woman)? Explain.

   b. Explain how you've seen God's grace touch each part of your life—home, work, church, friends, and so on.

Put It into Practice

1. Spend some extended time meditating on how Christ has shown you grace in the past year, and then get together with a friend to discuss what you've pondered. Make sure to end your time together with a prayer of thanksgiving.

2. How can you become a more gracious person at your job? Brainstorm several ways to accomplish this, and then put each one into practice one at a time.

21

The Eye-Opener

Turn Your Eyes upon Jesus

1. Read Luke 10:25-37.

   a. What question did the teacher ask Jesus (v. 25)? For what reason do you think he asked the question?

   b. How did Jesus answer (vv. 26-28)? Do you think the teacher expected this answer? Explain.

   c. Why did the teacher ask his follow-up question (v. 29)? What was the purpose of the second question?

   d. Why do you think Jesus told a story in reply (vv. 30-35)?

   e. What question did Jesus ask the teacher (v. 36)?

   f. What answer did the teacher give (v. 37)? How did Jesus instruct him to apply his own answer?

2. Read Romans 12:9-21; 13:8-10.

   a. How does the first subject mentioned in this passage set the stage for the whole passage to follow (Romans 12:9)?

   b. List every practical instruction you see in verses 10-21. Which instructions are positive and which are negative? Why are both important?

   c. What is the one debt Christians are to have perpetually (13:8)? Why is this debt ongoing? How does this verse teach us to fulfill the law?

   d. What instruction in 13:10 summarizes the whole law? Why does it summarize it?

Reflect on the Book

1. "The priest and the Levite were bad neighbors because they refused to be good neighbors."

    a. What is a "bad neighbor"? How does he or she differ from a good neighbor?

    b. How do we sometimes "refuse" to be good neighbors? Why do we do this?

2. "No law will ever make you be a good neighbor, but real love can't keep you from being a good neighbor."

    a. How does real love make us into good neighbors?

    b. How can you be a good neighbor to someone you don't even like?

3. "A neighbor is not defined by color or creed; a neighbor is defined by nearest need."

    a. What needs do you see around you? How could you be a good neighbor to the people with those needs?

    b. What keeps us from being good neighbors? How can we get past these obstacles?

Put It into Practice

1. Flabbergast your neighbor by asking how you can become a better neighbor. And then totally shock him or her by actually doing what he or she suggests.

2. Walk through today looking for the needs all around you. Then begin making a concerted effort to meet whatever needs you can.

22

The Divine Auditor

Turn Your Eyes upon Jesus

1. Read Matthew 25:14-30.

   a. What does this parable teach us about the kingdom of God?

   b. Compare and contrast the activity of the three servants described in verses 15-18.

   c. What happened with the first servant when the master returned home (vv. 19-21)? How did the master react?

   d. What happened with the second servant (vv. 22-23)? How did the master react?

   e. What did the third servant say upon the master's return (vv. 24-25)? How did he believe differently from the other two servants?

   f. How did the master react to the third servant (vv. 26-28)? What rationale does the master give for his actions?

   g. How do verses 29-30 serve as a general summary of the whole lesson? What is the takeaway for Jesus's disciples?

2. Read 1 Corinthians 12:12-20; Colossians 4:17.

   a. How is the church like a human body (1 Corinthians 12:12-13)? What implications does this have for every member of the church?

   b. What argument does Paul make using an absurd illustration (vv. 14-17)? How does his illustration connect to life in the church?

c. Who has arranged the parts of the body (v. 18)? What is significant about this?

d. How does Paul's summary statement relate to both human bodies and the church (v. 20)?

e. What is Paul's instruction to a particular church member in Colossians 4:17? How does this instruction relate to the image of the church as a body? What does it suggest for each of us in the church?

Reflect on the Book

1. "Certain skills—learning to blend with other instruments, keeping up to tempo, learning to play louder or softer, following a conductor's lead—can be learned only by playing in a band or orchestra."

   a. If you have ever played in a band or orchestra or on a team, describe your experience.

   b. What life skills can be learned best as part of a larger group? Why?

2. "It's not how much you have that matters to Jesus; it's what you do with what you have that matters to him."

   a. Why does what you do with what you have matter to Jesus?

   b. Do you think Jesus is pleased with how you handle what you've been given? Explain.

3. "Success is exercising responsibility, opportunity, and using your abilities for the glory of God and the good of others."

   a. How do you try to live your life to the glory of God? What does this look like in practical terms?

   b. How are you using your abilities to benefit others?

Put It into Practice

1. On a sheet of paper, list the spiritual gifts you know you have. Next to each gift, list how you are using that gift in the service of others.

2. Spend some time dreaming about how God might be able to use you and your gifts to glorify him in some way that you haven't yet tried. What would keep you from reaching toward that vision? What steps might help you move in that direction? Take those steps!

23

A Better Financial Planner

Turn Your Eyes upon Jesus

1. Read Luke 12:13-21.

   a. What prompted this teaching of Jesus about money (v. 13)?

   b. What general warning did Jesus give in verse 15?

   c. Did the man in Jesus's parable have good or bad investments (vv. 16-17)?

   d. How did the man respond to the success of his investments (vv. 18-19)? Did he show wisdom in his response? Explain.

   e. How did God respond to the man in verse 20? What was the man's core problem?

   f. How did Jesus summarize his lesson for the man who asked him the question (v. 21)?

2. Read 2 Corinthians 8:1-15.

   a. Why did Paul want to tell the Corinthians about the Macedonian church (vv. 1-4)? What prompted his report?

   b. What especially surprised the apostle about the Macedonians (v. 5)?

   c. What did Paul urge the Corinthians to do (v. 7)? In what way was this a gentle reminder, not a new request?

   d. Did Paul see this request as a command or a test (v. 8)? What's the difference between the two?

   e. How did Paul summarize the ministry of Jesus in verse 9?

    f. How did the apostle urge his friends to complete the work they pledged to do (vv. 10-12)?

    g. How is "equality" the main emphasis of verses 13-15? How did Paul use this idea to urge his friends to generosity?

Reflect on the Book

1. "We need only three things to live: shelter, food, and clothing. Everything else is wealth."

    a. By this definition, how wealthy are you?

    b. How would it change the way you live if you thought of yourself as wealthy?

2. "The man saw his money, his land, and his income as what he earned rather than what God had given."

    a. Do you see your income as what you have earned or what God has given you? Explain.

    b. When someone sees possessions as what they've earned rather than what God has given them, how does that change the way they live?

3. "Most people think that what they have is for them."

    a. Do you agree with this statement? Explain.

    b. If what you have is not for you, then who is it for?

Put It into Practice

1. Take an hour to review your checkbook or bank account statement. What does your review tell you about your use of money? What does it say about your view of money?

2. Find a worthwhile charity based in your home town and start giving to it. Start learning more about that charity and become an expert in what it does and how it does it.

24

The God of Tomorrow

Turn Your Eyes upon Jesus

1. Read Luke 16:1-13.

   a. Describe how Jesus set up his story in verses 1-2.

   b. How does the unscrupulous manager respond to his master's demand (vv. 3-7)? What is his basic plan of survival?

   c. How does the master react when he hears about the manager's plan (v. 8)? How can he commend the manager's cleverness without endorsing his misconduct?

   d. How did Jesus apply the story in verse 9?

   e. What general principle did Jesus lay out in verses 10-12? How does it relate to the parable?

   f. What overarching teaching axiom did Jesus develop in verse 13? How does this axiom relate to all of life?

2. Read Romans 14:10-12.

   a. Why did the apostle discourage us from judging each other (v. 10)?

   b. What promise was recalled in verse 11? How does this promise affect every person who ever lived?

   c. How did Paul summarize his teaching in verse 12? How is that summary intended to affect our day-to-day lives?

Reflect on the Book

1. "One day we will have to give an account for our accounts."

   a. For what accounts will you have to give an account?

    b. If you had to give an account today for your accounts, would you feel confident or fearful? Explain.

2. "The owner did not commend the steward for *what* he had done, but for *how* he had done it."

    a. In your own words, for what did the owner commend the crooked steward?

    b. What lesson can we learn from *how* the steward conducted his business?

3. "One day you are going to lose [everything you have], so use it today to get ready for tomorrow."

    a. How can you use your assets today to get ready for tomorrow?

    b. How can you make sure you control your assets rather than allowing them to control you?

Put It into Practice

1. It never hurts to sharpen your skills at handling money. Find a good, current book on effective resource management and work your way through it. Look especially for tips that can help you improve your current financial management.

2. Try an experiment: Set aside $100 and see how you can make those funds grow over the next year. At the end of the year, either give the whole amount to a worthy charity or give part of it away and do the whole thing again.

25

The Life of the Party

Turn Your Eyes upon Jesus

1. Read Luke 15:1-7.

   a. Why do you think Jesus attracted the kinds of crowds that so often surrounded him?

   b. What did the religious leaders think of Jesus's audience (v. 2)?

   c. Why might Jesus tell this kind of parable to an antagonistic audience? Why might a story work better than didactic teaching?

   d. What is the main point of the parable? What did Jesus want to emphasize? Why did he want to emphasize this particular point to this particular audience?

2. Read 1 Corinthians 9:16-23.

   a. Why did Paul say he preached (v. 16)?

   b. What is the "reward" Paul wanted to receive for preaching (vv. 17-18)?

   c. How did Paul customarily adapt himself to changing audiences (vv. 19-22)? Why did he say he conducted himself in this way?

   d. What was the overarching reason Paul conducted his ministry as he did (v. 23)?

Reflect on the Book

1. "Good shepherds don't care about *some* of the flock or even *most* of the flock. They care about *all* of the flock."

a. Why does this description apply especially to Jesus?

b. Imagine you are a shepherd. What problems arise for you because you have to care about *all* of the flock rather than some or most of it?

2. "When you view a person who is far from God in the same way that you see a child who is lost, your attitude and priorities toward them will change completely."

a. If you ever got lost as a child, describe what happened. What did you feel?

b. How can you start viewing people who are far from God as if they were lost children?

3. "As we pursue the lost with the love of Christ, heaven rejoices."

a. What would it mean for you to "pursue the lost with the love of Christ"?

b. How do you think Jesus, the chief Shepherd, responds when a lost person comes to him for salvation? With that in mind, how can you more effectively partner with him in introducing people to God?

Put It into Practice

1. Who is the least likely candidate for salvation that you know of personally? Commit to praying for this person every day for the next month and ask God to do something special either in his or her heart or in yours . . . or in both.

2. Do a short study on the duties of a US ambassador. What does he do? For what is she responsible? What does he have to learn? To whom does she report? Then make a comparison to the duties of a Christian ambassador for Jesus.

26

A Hospitable Host

Turn Your Eyes upon Jesus

1. Read Luke 14:12-24.

   a. What instruction did Jesus give his host in verses 12-14? Name both the positive and negative reasons he offered.

   b. What prompted Jesus to tell another parable (v. 15)?

   c. What elements of Jesus's story set up the conflict at the end (vv. 16-20)? Why would the hearers of the story probably have been scandalized by the behavior of the invited guests?

   d. How did the master respond to the news (v. 21)?

   e. How do verses 22-23 heighten the drama of the story?

   f. What is the purpose of the final line in verse 24? What point was Jesus trying to make at the real-life banquet he was attending?

2. Read 2 Corinthians 5:20–6:2.

   a. How did Paul describe himself and his companions in verse 20? Who was he representing? What was his goal and purpose?

   b. Who is the "him" of verse 21? What did he do for us? How did he accomplish this?

   c. What did Paul plead for his readers to do? What did he not want them to do?

   d. When is the "time of [God's] favor" (6:2 NIV)? When is the day of salvation? What does this imply?

Reflect on the Book

1. "The kingdom of God was not something that they were to be looking for *tomorrow*, it was already present in Jesus."

    a. In what way was the kingdom already present in Jesus?

    b. If you are in Christ, how is the kingdom already present in you?

2. "To reject God's gracious invitation dishonors the One who loved you enough to send his Son to die for you."

    a. In your experience, how have you seen people reject God's invitation?

    b. List some reasons why God's invitation is "gracious."

3. "We've all been given a far greater invitation to sit at the table of the Creator of the universe, the King of kings and the Lord of lords, and to enjoy his presence forever."

    a. What do you most look forward to in enjoying God's presence forever? What aspect of his company do you most anticipate?

    b. What do you think you might say to Jesus when you first see him face-to-face?

Put It into Practice

1. Set aside some time for extended prayer, thanking God for his gracious invitation to you to become part of his family.

2. Take a piece of paper and a pen or pencil and try to fill up the sheet with examples of how God has shown his grace to you in the last year.

27

The Object of Our Worship

Turn Your Eyes upon Jesus

1. Read Luke 18:9-14.

   a. To whom did Jesus tell this parable (v. 9)?

   b. Who are the two main characters in this story (vv. 10-13)? Describe each one.

   c. What big surprise did Jesus reveal at the end of his story (v. 14)? What kind of impact do you think that "reveal" had on Jesus's audience?

   d. What general principle does Jesus connect to his story (v. 14)?

2. Read Romans 12:3.

   a. Why did Paul mention "grace" at the beginning of his thought in this verse?

   b. What did Paul instruct believers *not* to do?

   c. What did Paul instruct believers to do instead?

   d. How does the apostle's instruction relate thematically to Jesus's parable above?

Reflect on the Book

1. "Do you ever look at people who don't go to church and think you are better than they are, because you do go to church?"

   a. Answer the question above and explain your answer.

   b. What are some reasons you've heard for why people don't go to church? What do you think of those answers?

2. "When you look up to God, you will never look down on others."

    a. What does it mean to look up to God?

    b. When are you most tempted to look down on people? How can you combat this?

3. "You will see yourself correctly only when you see God correctly."

    a. How has your picture of God changed over the last few years?

    b. Has your view of yourself changed as your picture of God has changed? Explain.

Put It into Practice

1. Write down as many reasons as you can think of for why it is foolish to compare yourself with others.

2. Whom do you tend to look down on? What kind of people do you often regard as inferior or loathsome? Spend some time in prayer asking God to forgive you and to help you change.

28

The Grace Giver

Turn Your Eyes upon Jesus

1. Read 2 Chronicles 33:9-23.

    a. How does the writer portray King Manasseh (v. 9)?

    b. How did God respond to the situation (v. 10)? How did the people respond to God?

    c. How did God finally respond to the king's intransigence (v. 11)?

    d. How did the king react to what had happened to him (v. 12)?

    e. How did God respond to the king, despite Manasseh's previous evil (v. 13)?

    f. How did Manasseh behave once God restored him (vv. 15-16)?

    g. How had the people, and the king's own son, been conditioned by his previous evil lifestyle choices (vv. 17, 22-23)? What lessons can we draw from this account?

2. Read Luke 15:11-32.

    a. Describe each of the three main characters in this story. Which do you most resemble? Explain.

    b. What word do you think best describes the younger son? Why?

    c. What word do you think best describes the older son? Why?

    d. What word do you think best describes the father? Why?

    e. Why do you think Jesus didn't conclude this story by

stating some general principle to summarize the main
point, as he often did?

Reflect on the Book

1. "The Father's door is always open and the Father's message is
   always 'welcome.'"
   a. What does it mean that the Father's door is always open?
   b. How does God make it clear that people are always
      welcome to come to him?

2. "Love doesn't care what other people think."
   a. Why doesn't love care what other people think?
   b. If you didn't care what other people thought, what God-
      inspired thing would you do?

3. "While the older brother is into punishment, the father is
   into pardon. The older brother is into guilt, but the father
   is into grace. The older brother is into revenge, but the
   father is into reconciliation."
   a. Why do you think the older brother was into
      punishment, guilt, and revenge?
   b. Why was the father into pardon, grace, and
      reconciliation?
   c. Which of these things are you into? Explain.

Put It into Practice

1. Ask your friends and acquaintances this week where they
   have experienced grace.

2. Ask three of your closest friends whether you most resemble
   the younger brother, the older brother, or the father in Jesus's
   story. And then take appropriate action in your own life.

29

Discerner of the Heart

Turn Your Eyes upon Jesus

1. Read Matthew 13:24-30.

   a. What is the connection between the kingdom of God and a man who sowed good seed in his field (v. 24)?

   b. What happens to the man's field (vv. 25-26)?

   c. What do the servants think they should do (v. 28)?

   d. What is the man's solution to his problem (vv. 29-30)? How is this solution meant to guide us as to how we are to conduct ourselves in a world where evil often masquerades as good?

2. Read Matthew 24:37-44.

   a. What comparisons did Jesus make between Noah's generation and the generation alive at the time he returns (vv. 37-39)?

   b. What was the main point of the sudden takings Jesus described (vv. 40-41)? How were they supposed to affect Jesus's hearers?

   c. What was Jesus's main point in this passage (v. 42)? What, in particular, did he want his disciples to do?

   d. What story did Jesus tell to highlight his main point (v. 43)? How did the story do this?

   e. Why did Jesus reemphasize his main point (v. 44)?

Reflect on the Book

1. "Just as [Stradivari] transformed trash into treasure, only God can transform you into what you were truly meant to be."

    a. Where have you seen God transform "trash" into "treasure"?

    b. What "trashy" areas of your life would you like to see God transform into treasure?

2. "Satan is not an innovator; he is an imitator. His counterfeits are people."

    a. Why do you think Satan is not an innovator?

    b. In what way does Satan counterfeit people? (See 2 Corinthians 11:14.)

3. "It's God's job to take the sinners from the saints."

    a. What problems do we cause when *we* try to take the sinners from the saints?

    b. How have you seen God take the sinners from the saints? How will he do it at the very end of history?

Put It into Practice

1. Take a cup of salt and mix it thoroughly in a bowl with a cup of sugar. Now try to separate the two ingredients. What troubles do you encounter?

2. See if you can track down an image of a counterfeit bill, whether at a museum or online. What distinguishes the counterfeit from the real?

30

A Divine Divider

Turn Your Eyes upon Jesus

1. Read Luke 16:19-31.

    a. How is the rich man described (v. 19)?

    b. How is the poor man described (vv. 20-21)?

    c. What happens to both men (v. 22)?

    d. How do the men's respective fortunes change after death (vv. 23-26)?

    e. What second request does the rich man make (vv. 27-28)?

    f. How does Abraham respond to this request (v. 29)?

    g. Why does the rich man continue to insist on his request (v. 30)?

    h. Why does Abraham continue to refuse the request (v. 31)?

    i. What insight sticks with you the most from this story? Why?

2. Read 2 Corinthians 5:9-11.

    a. What did Paul make his "goal" (v. 9 NIV)?

    b. What did Paul refer to as his primary motivation for pursuing this goal (v. 10)?

    c. Since Paul feared the Lord, what did he choose to do (v. 11)?

    d. If you were to stand before the judgment seat of Christ tonight, would you be ready? Explain.

Reflect on the Book

1. "What we do get to determine is how we leave this world."

    a. In what way do we get to determine how we leave this world?

    b. What would you like to leave behind when you leave this world?

2. "Today's decision determines tomorrow's destiny."

    a. What decisions are you making today that will have a long-term impact on your future?

    b. What big decisions have you made in the past that you wish you had made differently? How can you avoid making similar decisions today?

3. "Begin now to live for God, look to God, and listen to God, for that is the only life that will matter both today and tomorrow."

    a. Describe what it would look like for you to: (a) *live* for God, (b) *look* to God, and (c) *listen* to God.

    b. Imagine how you'll see your life after having lived in heaven for a thousand years. What are you worrying about today that you won't care about in the slightest then?

Put It into Practice

1. Do some research to determine what is involved in the process of making your will. Start now to think about all the issues a will must cover—and as you do, think more deeply about the kind of legacy you want to leave behind.

2. Think back on the last six "big" decisions you made. How did you make them? What process did you go through? Did you discuss them with anyone? Are you satisfied with those decisions? Pray about your general process of making decisions and ask the Lord to reveal any areas where you may need to make changes.

31

Flying Standby

Turn Your Eyes upon Jesus

1. Read Matthew 7:1-5.

    a. What is the difference between proper judgment and improper judgment? What guidelines could help you maintain the first and avoid the second?

    b. How would God judge you at this moment, if he were to judge you in the same way you have judged others?

    c. Why do we tend to look at the speck in our brother's eye while we ignore the log in our own?

    d. What plank (or planks) do you think you may have to remove from your own eye?

2. Read Romans 14:1-9.

    a. How would you define a "disputable matter" (v. 1 NIV)?

    b. Why would a weak faith be illustrated by a person who is allowed to eat only vegetables (v. 2)? What, other than dietary considerations, prevents the person from eating?

    c. In what areas of the contemporary church is it common for church people to "look down on" someone for engaging in some "disputable" practice (see v. 3 NIV)?

    d. Who is the master of the servant mentioned in verse 4? Why should this change our attitude? Who is able to make this servant "stand"?

    e. Why is it important to be "fully convinced" in your own mind on disputable matters that touch your own life (v. 5 NIV)?

    f. How can we dedicate whatever we do to the Lord (vv. 6-8)? If we cannot dedicate something wholeheartedly to the Lord, why would we be better to leave it alone?

    g. For what reason did Christ die and rise to life again, according to verse 9? What does this have to do with improperly judging others?

Reflect on the Book

1. "We've all sat in the seat of the judge, and we've all sat in the seat of the judged."

    a. Describe a time when you sat in the seat of the judge.

    b. Describe a time when you sat in the seat of the judged.

2. "There is a difference between confronting a sin and condemning a sinner."

    a. What is the difference between confronting a sin and condemning a sinner?

    b. Describe a time when someone effectively confronted you about something amiss in your life. What happened?

3. "A hypocrite is someone who looks out the window but never looks in the mirror."

    a. In your own words, describe the meaning of this sentence.

    b. Do you more often tend to look out the window or look in the mirror? Explain.

Put It into Practice

1. Imagine that you had to create a scene for a Hollywood movie about the judgment seat of Christ. What would your scene look like?

2. What are the most irritating sins in others that you have to admit you also see in yourself? What can you do to avoid focusing on the splinter instead of taking out the plank?

32

A Prayer Warrior

Turn Your Eyes upon Jesus

1. Read Matthew 6:5-8.

   a. What is wrong about praying so that people notice you praying (v. 5)? What does God find so distasteful about it? What does Jesus mean that such pray-ers have received "their reward in full" (NIV)?

   b. What is better about praying "in secret" (v. 6)? How does the Father respond to such praying? Why?

   c. Why do pagans (or "Gentiles") think they will be heard because they pray many words? Why are Christians not to pray like that (v. 7)?

   d. If God already knows what we need, then why do you think we have to pray to receive those things (v. 8)?

2. Read James 5:13-18.

   a. What kinds of things are we encouraged to pray about in verses 13-15? How are we to pray about these things?

   b. What is the connection between effective prayer and confession of sin (v. 16)? What kind of person can offer powerful and effective prayer (NIV)? Who qualifies to be such a person of prayer?

   c. In what ways was Elijah just like us (vv. 17-18)? How did James use Elijah's example to encourage us to pray?

Reflect on the Book

1. "I know that prayer is supposed to be a dialogue, but it often feels like a monologue."

    a. Do you agree with this statement? Explain.

    b. When does prayer most often feel like a monologue to you? How do you respond?

2. "When you shut out the noise of this world, you maximize your ability to hear God."

    a. What are some ways you can shut out the noise of the world?

    b. How do you know when you've really heard from God?

3. "Prayer is not primarily about getting things *from* God; it's about spending time *with* God."

    a. Why do you think God connects prayer with our receiving things from him?

    b. Describe the times when you feel most connected to God during prayer.

Put It into Practice

1. Every day this week, try spending ten minutes more with God than you normally do.

2. Often we focus on spending more time with God rather than spending more *productive* time with God. Try something different in your prayer times this week—pray in a setting where you are less likely to become distracted, for instance. What happens?

33

Focused on the Father

Turn Your Eyes upon Jesus

1. Read Matthew 6:9-10.

    a. Why are we instructed to call God "our" Father?

    b. Why are we to focus on God as our *Father* when we pray?

    c. What does it mean to "hallow" God's name? What are we really praying for?

    d. In what ways are we to pray that God's kingdom comes?

    e. How is God's will done in heaven? What are we praying for when we ask that his will be done here on earth in the same way it is done in heaven?

2. Read Matthew 26:36-44.

    a. Why did Jesus ask his friends the disciples to spend time in prayer with him (vv. 36-38)? Is this also a pattern for you? Explain.

    b. What does Jesus's physical posture tell us about his attitude at this time (v. 39)? What "cup" was Jesus asking to be removed from him? Why did he pray, "if it be possible"?

    c. Why do you think the disciples had fallen asleep (vv. 40-41)? Do you think there was anything going on in the garden beyond physical weariness? Explain.

    d. Jesus did not pray exactly the same prayer he prayed

earlier (v. 42). How was it different? How was it the same? What significance does this have, if any?

e. Why did Jesus continue to pray the same thing (v. 44)? How can this be instructive for our own prayer lives?

Reflect on the Book

1. "I often ask myself, *Will the prayer that I am about to pray honor God's name?*"

   a. What does it mean for you to "honor God's name" in your prayers?

   b. How would your prayer life change if you started asking yourself, "Will the prayer that I am about to pray honor God's name?"?

2. "The number one priority of prayer is not to get God to do what you want, but to get God to do what he wants."

   a. Why should we have to pray that God would do what he wants to do? Why wouldn't he just do it?

   b. What does it take for you to align your desires with God's will?

3. "Before you get to your wants, your desires, your agenda, you have to go to God and say, 'I want your will to be done.'"

   a. How does God let you know when your will is not his will?

   b. Describe a time when, through prayer, your will changed to align with God's will. What happened?

Put It into Practice

1. Think of an area in your life in which you believe you know God's will, but you struggle with accepting it. Seek out two

or three friends this week and ask them to pray for you regarding this specific issue.

2. What can you do to honor the name of God this week? Pick one thing—something you don't normally do—in your work, at your home, in your community, and in your church, and do it.

34

The One Who Provides

Turn Your Eyes upon Jesus

1. Read Matthew 6:11-15.

   a. When we ask God to give us our "daily bread," are we asking for more than bread alone (v. 11)? Why are we to ask for these things every day?

   b. Why do you think Jesus connected *our* forgiveness with our forgiving *others* (v. 12)?

   c. How often do we lead ourselves into temptation? What are we asking God to do when we ask him not to lead us into temptation (especially given James 1:13)?

   d. Name a few specific ways, appropriate to your life, in which you could ask God to deliver you from the evil one.

   e. Why do you think Jesus mentions the necessity of forgiving others once more, immediately after he finishes his model prayer (vv. 14-15)? Why are forgiveness and prayer so closely bound together?

2. Read Philippians 4:4-7.

   a. Why do you think rejoicing is so often connected with our praying (v. 4)?

   b. Why is it necessary to go into prayer with the right attitude (v. 5)? Why is it important to remember that the Lord is "at hand"? What does it mean that he is near?

c. In what way is prayer intended to be an antidote to anxiety (v. 6)? How does Spirit-filled prayer combat worry? Why do you think Paul includes "thanksgiving" with his instructions on prayer? What kind of requests are we to offer to God?

d. How is prayer designed to affect our emotional state (v. 7)? How is prayer to affect both the heart and the mind? How does it affect the heart differently than it does the mind?

Reflect on the Book

1. "We pray because we have problems that only God can solve, questions that only God can answer, and needs that only God can meet."

   a. What problems do you have that only God can solve?

   b. What questions do you have that only God can answer?

   c. What needs do you have that only God can meet?

2. "The words 'give us' remind us what our relationship to God is actually like: we are completely dependent on him and he is completely independent of us."

   a. Why do you think God made us completely dependent on him?

   b. How does it make you feel that God is completely independent of us? Explain.

3. "If you're not willing to forgive the debts of others, you are actually asking God not to forgive you."

   a. What do we reveal about ourselves when we are unwilling to forgive someone else?

   b. How does a refusal to forgive indicate a completely anti-God state of mind?

Put It into Practice

1. Write to a missionary family and ask how you can pray for their "daily bread."

2. Ask your pastor if you could pray for some problem that is especially vexing either the church or someone he loves, and commit to doing it each day this week.

35

The Treasure Principle

Turn Your Eyes upon Jesus

1. Read Matthew 6:19-24.

   a. What kinds of items are we instructed not to "store up" (v. 19 NIV)? What is the problem with storing up these sorts of items?

   b. What kinds of items are we instructed to store up (v. 20)? How does one store up these things? How can we store up things in heaven while we still live on earth?

   c. What do you consider your greatest treasure (v. 21)? Where do you spend most of your time, or what would you be most heartbroken to lose? What does that say about where your heart is?

   d. What kind of "eyes" and "light" does Jesus have in mind in verses 22-23? What kind of "light" do you think you have within yourself? Explain.

   e. Why is it impossible to "serve" both God and money (v. 24)? What does it mean to serve money? Why does Jesus say that if you "love" the one, you will "despise" the other?

2. Read 1 Timothy 6:17-19.

   a. Why is it easy for the rich to get "haughty" (v. 17)? Why is it easy to put your hope in wealth? Why is wealth "uncertain" (NIV)? How do you put your hope in God? Why does God supply us with the things we need, according to verse 17?

    b. What four things does verse 18 command rich people to do? How are they related to one another? How are they distinct?

    c. What reason for his command did Paul give in verse 19? What promise did he relay? What benefit did he describe?

Reflect on the Book

1. "Jesus talked more about money than he talked about heaven and hell combined."

    a. Why do you think Jesus talked so much about money?

    b. What do your own conversations about money usually involve?

2. "You cannot divorce your faith and your finances."

    a. Why is it impossible to divorce your faith from your finances?

    b. How do we often try to divorce our faith from our finances?

3. "Once you understand the Treasure Principle and how to apply it in your life, you will experience real financial freedom and a joy in your life like you never have before."

    a. Describe the Treasure Principle in your own words.

    b. How does the Treasure Principle help us to experience both joy and financial freedom?

Put It into Practice

1. For one month, keep track of all the nonessential "little" things you buy that cost under $10.00—impulse items, candy, beverages, and the like. Are you surprised by the amount?

2. Figure out what percentage of your income you give to church and other charitable organizations. How does this percentage compare to what you gave five years ago? Are you satisfied with the results? If not, make a plan to change.

36

A Marriage Counselor

Turn Your Eyes upon Jesus

1. Read Genesis 2:18-25.

   a. What was the first thing in the garden declared to be "not good" (v. 18)? What was not good about it? What was God's solution for this "not good" situation?

   b. Why would God cause all the animals to pass before Adam before addressing the "not good" situation of verse 18 (vv. 19-20)? What lesson was he trying to convey?

   c. How did God form the woman he made for man (vv. 21-22)? Why do it in this way? Why not form her out of the same earth from which Adam had been formed?

   d. How did Adam respond to this new companion (v. 23)? If he were to put these thoughts in modern language, what do you think he might say?

   e. For what "reason" will a man leave his father and mother (v. 24)? Why is it necessary to leave? What does it mean to be "united" to one's spouse (NIV)? In what way are they "one flesh"?

   f. Why does the writer tell us Adam and Eve felt no shame (v. 25)? What is the point of that declaration?

2. Read Matthew 19:3-9.

   a. Why is it significant that some Pharisees came to test Jesus about his views on divorce (v. 3)?

   b. To what did Jesus immediately point his questioners (vv. 4-5)? Why should this always be our first recourse?

   c. According to Jesus, who joins a man and woman in

marriage (v. 6)? What should be unbreakable about that joining?

d. Where do Jesus's questioners immediately point after they hear his answer (v. 7)? What do they hope he will say?

e. Note that while the Pharisees used the word "command" in verse 7, Jesus used the word "allow" (v. 8). Why did he make this distinction? Why did he take his discussion all the way back to the beginning?

f. What one exception did Jesus mention in verse 9? Did he "command" divorce in these situations? Explain.

Reflect on the Book

1. "Instead of answering the question, 'How can you get *out* of a marriage?' Jesus answered the question, 'Why should you stay *in* a marriage?'"

   a. Why did Jesus say married people should stay in their marriages?

   b. Why do you think Jesus spoke about marriage when he was asked about divorce?

2. "The preeminent relationship in a family is not between a child and a parent, but between a husband and a wife."

   a. Why is the preeminent relationship in a family the one between a husband and a wife?

   b. What often happens when married couples put their children before their own marital relationship?

3. "As the two who've become one look to the One who invented marriage, what God has joined together, God can *keep* together."

   a. How can a strong mutual commitment to God keep a marriage together?

   b. Why do you think God is so pro-marriage and anti-divorce?

Put It into Practice

1. If you are married, plan a weekend away with your spouse where the two of you make some specific plans about what you want to accomplish as a family this year. If you are single, set aside a day during which you can do this.

2. Many studies show that couples that habitually pray together tend to have longer and more satisfying marriages. If the two of you don't often pray together, get started today. Start out with just five minutes together, at a set time and place.

37

Can One Become Two?

Turn Your Eyes upon Jesus

1. Read Matthew 19:10-12.

   a. How did the disciples react to Jesus's teaching on divorce and remarriage (v. 10)? Why do you think they reacted in this way?

   b. What "word" cannot everyone "accept" (v. 11 NIV)? To whom has this word particularly been given?

   c. How does the word *for* connect verses 11 and 12? What did Jesus have in mind when he spoke of a "eunuch"? What were the two primary ways that Jesus said men became eunuchs? Why would someone "renounce" marriage because of the "kingdom of heaven"? How do we know that the "word" not everyone can accept is choosing not to marry?

2. Read 1 Corinthians 7:10-17.

   a. How do verses 10-11 compare with Jesus's instruction on marriage? What related instruction does this passage give?

   b. What further instruction does Paul give in verses 12-13? How is this instruction consistent with what was given before? Why was the additional instruction necessary?

   c. What encouragement does verse 14 give Christians in mixed marriages? What promise was given? How was this promise designed to set their minds at ease?

   d. What circumstance changes in verse 15? How did that

circumstance change Paul's instruction? Why did he remind us we are called to "peace"?

e. What possibility did Paul have in mind in verse 16? Why is this an additional reason for mixed couples to stay together?

f. How does Paul connect the ideas of a place "assigned" to believers and a place to which they have been "called," in regard to marriage (v. 17)?

Reflect on the Book

1. "Jesus's attitude toward marriage is *one and done*."

   a. Why do you think divorce is so rampant, even among Christians?

   b. What do you think can help Christian couples to refrain from seeing divorce as a solution to their problems?

2. "If you divorce for any reason other than sexual immorality on the part of your spouse, and you remarry someone else, you commit adultery."

   a. Do you agree with the statement above? Explain.

   b. Why do you think God is so appalled by adultery?

3. "Experts say that the three key components for holding a marriage together are:

   • Make up your mind to stay with it.

   • Actively work on the relationship.

   • Focus on your own behavior and attitude, not that of your spouse."

   a. Which of the three elements above do you find easiest? Explain.

   b. Which of the three elements above do you find hardest? Explain.

   c. Which of the three elements above do you need to work on the most? Explain.

Put It into Practice

1. Speak to a pastor who does marriage counseling, and ask about the emotional impact of divorce on families. You could also ask children of divorce about this.

2. Talk to several friends who have gone through a divorce and discuss with them the toll it took on them. Ask them if they believe there is anything they could have done to prevent heading down the path to divorce.

38

Love: Can Two Stay One?

Turn Your Eyes upon Jesus

1. Read John 13:34-35.

   a. Why did Jesus call this a "new" command (v. 34)? In what way has Jesus loved us? How is that kind of love to provide guidance for how we are to love one another?

   b. What did Jesus claim is the single best testimony to non-Christians that we are his disciples (v. 35)?

2. Read Galatians 5:13-15.

   a. What contrast does verse 13 set up? How does this verse combine thoughts on freedom, choice, service, and love? How does this train of thought relate to marriage?

   b. How does the command to love your neighbor sum up the entire law?

   c. What warning does Paul give in verse 15? Is this a word for marriage? Explain.

Reflect on the Book

1. "There is a big difference between falling in love and staying in love. One takes a pulse and the other takes a commitment."

   a. What do you think it means to "fall in love"? Why does it take only a "pulse"?

   b. What do you think it requires to stay in love? What is involved in that kind of commitment?

2. "You cannot *command* a feeling—but Jesus does command us to love."

   a. Why is it impossible to command a feeling?

   b. What is Jesus commanding us to do when he commands us to love?

3. "Whatever else is said about you, your spouse, and your marriage, let your children and grandchildren, friends, relatives, and neighbors say, 'Behold! How they love one another.'"

   a. If you're married, how can you more effectively love your spouse? If you're not married, what would you consider key ways to love your spouse?

   b. Think of the most loving couple you know. What gives them such love for one another?

Put It into Practice

1. If you don't know the specific "love language" of your spouse, go to this website and begin to find out: http://www.5lovelanguages.com/profile/.

2. As a couple, pick a good book on marriage and go through it together.

39

The Number One Priority

Turn Your Eyes upon Jesus

1. Read Matthew 6:25-34.

   a. What items did Jesus specify in verse 25 that are not to be objects of our worry? What question did he ask? Why did he ask this question? What answer did he expect? Why would this answer help to combat our anxieties?

   b. What examples did Jesus give in verses 26-30 to illustrate his teaching in verse 25?

   c. What negative reason did Jesus give in verse 31 for refusing to indulge in worry? What positive reason did he give?

   d. What command was given in verse 33? What corresponding promise was given?

   e. What further reasons did Jesus give us for refusing to worry (v. 34)?

2. Read Matthew 22:34-40.

   a. Describe the background that prompted the question asked of Jesus (v. 34).

   b. What do you suppose the lawyer was trying to get Jesus to say? What was the nature of this "test"?

   c. Why do you think that, although Jesus was asked to name one commandment, he named two? Why not stop at one? What do you think he was trying to get the lawyer to see?

   d. How do "all" the Law and the Prophets "depend" on these two commandments?

Reflect on the Book

1. "Ultimately, the sum total of your life will be determined by what you choose to make your greatest priority."

   a. What are your four greatest priorities in life?

   b. How does your life reflect each of these priorities?

2. "The key to getting what you need out of life is to focus on what Jesus wants for your life."

   a. What do you think Jesus wants for your life, in particular?

   b. What in your life do you need that you don't currently have?

3. "If my number one priority in life is to seek God's kingdom and God's righteousness, then everything I do can be ordered by two things...'Is this for his kingdom? Does it relate to his righteousness?'"

   a. How is a central concern for Jesus's kingdom reflected in your home life, your career, your social life, and your church life?

   b. How is a central concern for Jesus's righteousness reflected in your use of money, your use of media, your relationships, and your planning for the future?

Put It into Practice

1. Divide a piece of paper into two columns. On one side write what you believe to be your top five priorities. On the other side write how you spend most of your time. How do the two sides line up?

2. Have a family meeting in which you discuss together what you believe to be God's purpose for your family.

40

The Thirst Quencher

Turn Your Eyes upon Jesus

1. Read John 4:4-42.

   a. How did Jesus use a personal request to reach the place where he could give rather than receive (vv. 7-9)?

   b. Why did Jesus use a term that might be misunderstood ("living water") to spark a deeper spiritual interest (v. 10)? What can we learn from this?

   c. How many times in this passage did Jesus either ignore the woman's questions or deflect them? How did he do this? Why did he do this?

   d. What did Jesus mean when he told the woman she worshiped what she did not know (v. 22)? Do you think he risked offending her? Explain.

   e. What direct claim did Jesus make in verse 26?

   f. What things did Jesus actually tell the woman? Why did she say he told her everything she ever did (v. 29)?

   g. What is the "work" Jesus was doing that he considered "food" (vv. 32, 34)?

   h. What "harvest" did Jesus want his disciples to see (v. 35)?

   i. How did Jesus describe the spiritual sowing and reaping process (vv. 36-38)? What can we learn for our own evangelism efforts from this?

   j. In what way did the woman become a more effective evangelist than the disciples (vv. 39-42)? What do you

think made her such an effective evangelist? What can
we learn from her?

2. Read Acts 10:23-48.

   a. Why did Cornelius fall at Peter's feet (v. 25)? Why did
Peter make him get up (v. 26)?

   b. Why do you think Peter stated the rule against Jews
associating or visiting Gentiles (v. 28)?

   c. Why did Peter believe God had sent him to speak the
gospel message to Cornelius (vv. 34-35)?

   d. Why do you think the Holy Spirit fell on Cornelius and
his friends even as Peter was still speaking (v. 44)?

   e. How did this event convince Peter that the gospel was
for all people, regardless of their background?

Reflect on the Book

1. "Jesus is not the least bit bothered by who you are, what
you've done, or what anybody else thinks of you."

   a. Are *you* bothered by who you are, what you've done, or
what others think of you? Explain.

   b. How would your life change if you weren't bothered by
these things?

2. "Anybody, no matter what they've done or who they are, no
matter how bad they have messed up, can worship God if
they do it in spirit and in truth."

   a. What does it mean to worship God "in spirit"?

   b. What does it mean to worship God "in truth"?

3. "[Jesus] chose to go to an out-of-the-way town to extend
God's grace and love to an out-of-the-way woman—one who
discovered she'd been thirsty because she'd been drinking the
wrong kind of water."

a. What "out of-the-way" men and women do you know? How can you show them God's grace and love?

b. How can you tell when someone is thirsty for spiritual water?

Put It into Practice

1. Jesus was a master at using questions to pique someone's interest. Over the next few days, concentrate on asking questions of people to see if you can draw them out.

2. Jesus spoke of "living water" to a woman who came to draw water from a well. Look around at the physical objects surrounding you and try to think of creative ways to use them in your conversations to introduce the topic of faith.

41

A Most Valuable Treasure

Turn Your Eyes upon Jesus

1. Read Mark 10:17-31.

   a. How can you tell that this man was serious about his question, and not simply trying to trap Jesus in some kind of test (v. 17)?

   b. Why did Jesus focus the man's attention on his use of the word *good* (v. 18)?

   c. Why do you think John reported that Jesus looked at the man "and loved him" (v. 21)?

   d. Why is it so hard for rich people to enter the kingdom of God (vv. 23-25)?

   e. How is verse 27 designed to give hope to rich people (and to everyone else)?

   f. What contrast was Peter trying to make in verse 28? Why did he want to make this contrast?

   g. What promise did Jesus make in verses 29-30? What sobering reality accompanies that promise?

   h. How does verse 31 wrap up the lesson?

2. Read Philippians 3:3-11.

   a. How much "confidence" did Paul put "in the flesh" (v. 3)?

   b. Why should Paul have been able to put a great deal of confidence in the flesh (vv. 4-6)? List each of his reasons.

   c. Why would Paul consider the "loss" of many earthly

advantages to be great "gain" (vv. 7-9)? List each of his reasons.

d. In your own words, describe Paul's greatest life ambition (vv. 10-11).

Reflect on the Book

1. "Sacrifice is key to having a relationship with Christ."

   a. Why is sacrifice key to having a relationship with Christ? How do sacrifice and grace go together?

   b. How did the apostle Paul describe his own "sacrifices" in Philippians 3:4-8?

2. "If you want God in your heart, you've got to give your heart to God."

   a. What does it mean to give your heart to God?

   b. How does someone continually give his or her heart to God?

3. "Only when you surrender everything to Jesus can you avoid becoming the biggest loser and invite him to transform you into the biggest winner."

   a. What does it mean to "surrender everything to Jesus"?

   b. What would it mean for you, personally, to surrender everything to Jesus?

Put It into Practice

1. Invite one of your closest friends to tell you what he or she sees as the biggest obstacle to spiritual growth in your life.

2. Compile a list of all the benefits you see to being a Christian. Then meditate on this list over a period of time, and take time to thank God for the benefits you've enjoyed in him.

42

A Gracious Judge

Turn Your Eyes upon Jesus

1. Read John 8:3-11.

   a. How do you think the religious leaders were hoping Jesus would respond to their "test" (v. 6)?

   b. Without speculating on what Jesus may have written in the sand, why do you think he refused at first to answer their question (v. 6)?

   c. When Jesus finally spoke, he made a statement rather than answering any of their questions (v. 7). And then he started writing in the sand again. Why do you think he did that?

   d. Why do you think the older men went away first, not the younger men, after they "heard" (not "read") Jesus's words (v. 9)?

   e. What questions did Jesus ask the woman (v. 10)? Why ask her questions?

   f. What instruction did Jesus give the woman (v. 11)? How is this significant?

2. Read Titus 2:11-14.

   a. What does the grace of God do for us (v. 11)?

   b. What does the grace of God teach us to do (v. 12)? How does grace teach us these things?

   c. How should our belief about the Second Coming affect our life in this world (v. 13)?

d. Why did Jesus give himself for us, according to verse 14? Name two key reasons.

Reflect on the Book

1. "If you have any conscience at all, any character at all, when you are caught red-handed with no escape and no excuse, it will leave you broken."

    a. Why does getting caught red-handed tend to leave a person broken?

    b. Describe a time when you felt broken in this way. What happened?

2. "This woman is awaiting the verdict, which she knows will be *guilty*. But the Judge says, 'I don't condemn you.'"

    a. Why would an honest judge say, "I don't condemn you" to a guilty person?

    b. Why did Jesus tell the woman that he didn't condemn her?

3. "Jesus loves us just the way we are, but he loves us too much to let us stay that way."

    a. Why does Jesus not want us to stay the way we are, if he truly loves us?

    b. How do you think Jesus wants you to change in this next year?

Put It into Practice

1. Where do you most need help to grow in your spiritual life? Pick a faithful friend and ask him or her to help you develop a plan to start growing in that area.

2. Ponder this thought: The grace of God teaches us to say no to ungodliness. How does the grace of God teach you to say no to ungodliness? How can you better cooperate with the grace that's active in your life?

43

Always Available, Always Accessible

Turn Your Eyes upon Jesus

1. Read Mark 5:25-34.

    a. What did the woman feel when she touched Jesus's clothes (v. 29)?

    b. What did Jesus realize when the woman touched his clothes (v. 30)?

    c. Why do you think the woman tried to keep hidden for some time (vv. 32-33)?

    d. Which of the three things Jesus said to the woman— "Daughter," "go in peace," or "be freed from your suffering" (NIV)—do you think meant the most to her? Why?

2. Read Galatians 6:1-3.

    a. What instruction did Paul give to "spiritual" people who were dealing with someone caught in a sin (v. 1)? What does it mean to be a "spiritual" person? What instruction does he give them regarding themselves? Why give them this instruction?

    b. How can we "fulfill the law of Christ" (v. 2)? What is the law of Christ?

    c. How do we often deceive ourselves (v. 3)? How can we keep from deceiving ourselves in this way?

Reflect on the Book

1. "As we pattern our lives after Jesus, he brings us people who hurt so that we can offer them help and hope."

    a. How are you patterning your life after the life of Jesus?

    b. What people might Jesus bring to you so you can offer them help and hope?

2. "She needed the presence of someone in her life who was willing to take time out of their busy schedule to let her know 'I care about you' and 'I'll be here to help you.'"

    a. Think of someone who needs your care and help. How can you take time out of your busy schedule for this individual? How can you choose to be "with" this person?

    b. How do you let others know you care about them and that you're there to help them?

3. "You and I are called to...minister the grace, the love, and the power of Jesus Christ—to be the hem of his garment."

    a. In what ways are you most gifted to minister the grace, love, and power of Jesus to others?

    b. How can you be "the hem of his garment" to some needy individual today?

Put It into Practice

1. Find a way for your whole family to serve as "the hem of his garment." Consider volunteering some of your time at a shelter, a school, a food bank, or some other worthy organization in your area.

2. Find an old hymnal (or scour the Internet) and look for a dozen old hymns that talk about grace in a way that resonates with your heart.

44

Our Best Friend

Turn Your Eyes upon Jesus

1. Read Luke 19:1-10.

   a. What brought Zacchaeus out to see Jesus? General spiritual concern? Curiosity? Does it make a difference? Explain.

   b. How do you think Jesus knew the identity of Zacchaeus? What kind of a surprise do you think Zacchaeus received?

   c. Why do you think Zacchaeus welcomed Jesus "joyfully" (v. 6)?

   d. Why do you think the people grumbled (v. 7)?

   e. How could Jesus say that salvation had come to Zacchaeus's house (v. 9)?

   f. In your own words, describe Jesus's mission statement (v. 10).

2. Read 1 Corinthians 1:26-31.

   a. Why did Paul want the Corinthians to remember their unspectacular heritage (v. 26)?

   b. Why did God choose the "weak," "foolish," "low," and "despised" things of the world (vv. 27-29)? How does this make you feel? Explain.

   c. Why is anyone a Christian (v. 30)?

   d. Why is it always appropriate to boast "in the Lord" (v. 31)? What does it mean to boast in the Lord?

Reflect on the Book

1. "People who felt unloved by everybody else felt loved by Jesus."

    a. How did Jesus show love to those who felt unloved?

    b. How does Jesus show that he loves you?

2. "The more those who are not followers of Christ are loved by those of us who are followers of Christ, the more open they may be to following Christ."

    a. Is it hard for you to love those who don't follow Jesus? If so, what is difficult about it?

    b. Describe how you have seen men and women getting "loved into" the kingdom of Christ.

3. "When Jesus comes into your life, he not only makes you right with him, but he also makes you want to be right with others."

    a. What things changed in your life when Jesus made you right with him?

    b. How does Jesus prompt you to want to get right with others? Where do you currently have some challenging relationships that need to be made right?

Put It into Practice

1. Write a note of thanks to someone in the church who has shown you Christ's love during a difficult time.

2. The next time you are at church, look around to see if you can see someone who appears to be struggling. Even if you don't know the person well, sensitively investigate to see what you might be able to do to show that person Jesus's love.

45

The Standard of Greatness

Turn Your Eyes upon Jesus

1. Read Mark 9:33-37.

   a. If Jesus already knew what his disciples had been arguing about, why did he ask them?

   b. Why did Jesus's disciples not admit the truth?

   c. Jesus did not merely tell his disciples to serve or put themselves last. He framed his teaching within the idea, "If anyone wants to be first . . ." (v. 35 NIV). Why did he teach the lesson like this?

   d. What was the purpose of using the child as an object lesson (vv. 36-37)?

2. Read Philippians 2:3-11.

   a. What opposing frames of mind did Paul contrast in verse 3?

   b. What instruction did he give in verse 4?

   c. How can we develop the attitude Jesus had (vv. 5-6)?

   d. Describe the various aspects of Jesus's character that we are to emulate (vv. 6-8).

   e. Describe the reward Jesus will receive for living in this way (vv. 9-11). Why did Paul tell us about the future that is coming for Jesus?

Reflect on the Book

1. "There's a difference between doing great things and being a great person."

   a. How would you define "doing great things"? Can you name the greatest thing you've ever seen done?

   b. What is your definition of being a "great person"? Who's the greatest person you know?

2. "…you should know Jesus's secret to greatness. It's service."

   a. What is so great about service?

   b. What kind of servant are you? How would others describe your service?

3. "The world measures greatness by how many people serve you. Jesus measures greatness by how many people you serve."

   a. In a typical week, who do you serve? How willingly do you serve them?

   b. Who do you find it difficult to serve? Why?

Put It into Practice

1. Think of the single greatest service experience you've ever had. What was so great about it? How can you multiply that experience into others like it, or even greater experiences?

2. Offer to volunteer somewhere for a whole day where you'll likely have to do an unpleasant, thankless job. Rather than think of how disagreeable it is, consciously think of Jesus and his example of service. At the end of the day, thank God for the opportunity to serve.

46

A Servant First

Turn Your Eyes upon Jesus

1. Read John 13:1-17.

   a. In what way does this incident show the full extent of Jesus's love (v. 1)? What does this suggest about the connection between love and service?

   b. Why do you think John told us at the beginning of this account that Satan already had prompted Judas Iscariot to betray Jesus (v. 2)?

   c. What three significant things did John tell us about Jesus in verse 3? Why choose those particular three things as a preface to the Upper Room story?

   d. What did Jesus do in verses 4-5? Why was this surprising?

   e. How did Peter respond (vv. 6-8)? How did Jesus reply (vv. 7-8)? How did Peter react to this reply (v. 9)?

   f. What lesson did Jesus draw out of the incident for his disciples (vv. 12-17)? List as many distinct teaching points as you see.

2. Read Luke 12:35-38.

   a. What kind of attitude did Jesus say we should cultivate as a matter of habit (v. 35)?

   b. What story did Jesus use to illustrate the attitude he wants from us (v. 36)?

   c. What surprising reward did Jesus say awaits those who follow his instruction (vv. 37-38)?

Reflect on the Book

1. "More than anything else, Jesus desires two things from his followers: a surrendered heart and a servant spirit."

   a. How have you surrendered your heart to Jesus? How do you show this in day-to-day life?

   b. How do you demonstrate your servant spirit? What do you most enjoy about servanthood?

2. "When you surrender your dirty life to [Jesus], he bathes you in his grace and in his love and in his forgiveness. You are in his eyes completely clean."

   a. Do you feel "completely clean" in Jesus? Explain.

   b. What can you do when you don't feel completely clean?

3. "Once we surrender ourselves to him and admit we need him to wash us, only then will we see the opportunities, every day, to follow his example and to serve the needs of others."

   a. What does it look like for you to surrender your life to Jesus every day?

   b. When are you most likely to see opportunities to serve the needs of others? When are you most likely to take advantage of these opportunities?

Put It into Practice

1. If you think it might work in your family, stage a reenactment of the foot-washing episode of the Upper Room. Then, afterward, discuss it as a family.

2. Investigate what kind of service opportunities regularly go unfulfilled at your church. Pick one of them and serve the Lord in this way.

47

The Victor

Turn Your Eyes upon Jesus

1. Read Luke 4:1-13.

   a. Why do you think the Spirit chose to begin Jesus's earthly ministry with a forty-day temptation?

   b. Why do you suppose the devil began his first temptation with the word *if* (v. 3)?

   c. How did the devil use the word *if* in his second temptation (v. 7)?

   d. How did the devil use the word *if* in his third temptation (v. 9)? How did he misuse the Bible (v. 10)?

   e. After the temptations, the devil left Jesus until when (v. 13)? What might he have considered an "opportune time"?

2. Read Galatians 5:16-18.

   a. Describe a simple principle for avoiding the temptation of giving in to the lusts of the flesh (v. 16). What is an effective way for you to put this principle into practice?

   b. What makes living in a godly way so challenging for us (v. 17)?

   c. What is the problem with being "under the law" (v. 18)? What does it mean to be led by the Spirit? Describe your own experience of being led by the Spirit. What does this look like for you?

Reflect on the Book

1. "Even though temptation is going to come to all of us, we can also know that temptation does not have to defeat any of us."

   a. When does temptation tend to come to you the most?

   b. When have you had the most success at defeating temptation? How have you combatted it?

2. "The three specific ways that Satan tempted Jesus are the same three ways that Satan will tempt us." That is, the *physical*, the *emotional*, and the *spiritual*.

   a. What kind of *physical* temptations are most likely to confront you? How can you best deal with them?

   b. What kind of *emotional* temptations are most likely to confront you? How can you best deal with them?

   c. What kind of *spiritual* temptations are most likely to confront you? How can you best deal with them?

3. "Jesus had two secret weapons to fight temptation. And they're the same ones we have. Jesus was filled with the Spirit and he was armed with the Scriptures."

   a. Describe your experience of being filled with the Spirit. What does this look like for you?

   b. How do you spend time in the Scriptures? Describe your experience of interacting with the Bible.

Put It into Practice

1. Identify your top four temptations, and then put together a group of Scripture passages to combat each of them. Memorize these passages so you can immediately access them whenever you need their help.

2. Ask several Christian leaders you respect to recommend a good book on being filled with the Spirit. Decide on a title, get it, and read it.

48

Commander in Chief

Turn Your Eyes upon Jesus

1. Read Luke 9:23-26.

   a. What does it mean to "come after" Jesus (v. 23)? Who would want to do this? What does it look like?

   b. What does it mean to "deny" yourself? What does it mean to take up your cross every day? What does it mean to "follow" Jesus?

   c. What basic principle is given in verse 24? What does this mean in practical terms?

   d. Answer Jesus's question in verse 25.

   e. Why do you think Jesus mentioned shame in this passage (v. 26)? What is its connection to the rest of the passage?

2. Read Mark 12:28-34.

   a. Do you believe the teacher in this passage asked Jesus his question in order to trap him, like many other teachers? Explain.

   b. How did this teacher react to Jesus's answer in verses 32-33?

   c. What did Jesus mean in his response (v. 34)? What does it mean to be "not far" from the kingdom of God?

   d. Why did no one dare to ask Jesus any more questions after this incident?

Reflect on the Book

1. "The wholehearted Lord is not interested in halfhearted followers."

    a. What does the word *wholehearted* mean to you?

    b. Who is the most wholehearted believer you know? What makes this person so exceptional?

2. "If you haven't given up everything, you have already lost."

    a. What does this sentence mean? Do you agree with it? Explain.

    b. What things do you believe you may have to "give up" in order to receive God's best for you? Explain.

3. "If Jesus is going to live in you, you must die to you."

    a. What does it look like to die to yourself?

    b. Is dying to self a one-time event or a continual process? Explain.

Put It into Practice

1. Do a word study in the Bible on the term *wholehearted*. Who does the Bible call wholehearted? What characteristics do these people have? How can you become more wholehearted?

2. Divide a piece of paper into two columns. On one side write all the attractive things you believe you might have to give up if you were to follow Christ with a whole heart. On the other side write the things you would gain by giving yourself wholly to the Lord. Then compare the two sides.

49

The Passion of the Christ—the Rest of the Story

Turn Your Eyes upon Jesus

1. Read Luke 22:63–23:25.

   a. How did the guards mistreat Jesus (vv. 63-65)? What specifically did they do to him?

   b. What did the council want Jesus to tell them (v. 67)? Why did they want this information?

   c. How did Jesus reply to them (vv. 67-68)? What does he mean by his response in verse 68?

   d. Did the council understand his answer (vv. 70-71)? How do you know? Why did they think his response gave them all the information they needed to know?

   e. Describe Pilate's interaction with Jesus (23:1-7). Why did Pilate want to send Jesus to Herod?

   f. Describe Herod's interaction with Jesus (vv. 8-11). In what way did it significantly differ from Jesus's encounter with Pilate? Why the difference?

   g. What caused Pilate and Herod to become friends that day (v. 12)?

   h. Describe Pilate's second interaction with Jesus (vv. 13-25).

   i. What do you think Pilate hoped to accomplish by ordering Jesus's crucifixion?

2. Read 1 Peter 3:18.

   a. Why did Jesus have to die for our sins just once?

   b. What does it mean that Jesus was "righteous"? What does it mean that we were "unrighteous"?

c. Why did Jesus die? What was the purpose?

Reflect on the Book

1. "If Jesus was more than a man, if he *was* the Son of God, then there has never been another death like his."

   a. Thousands have died by crucifixion. What made Jesus's death so unique?

   b. What does it mean to you to have the Son of God in your life? What difference does it make?

2. "[Jesus] died not only for sin; he died *in place of* the sinner."

   a. Why did Jesus have to die in place of the sinner? Why couldn't God just forgive us without having Jesus go to the cross?

   b. What do you think it must have felt like for the sinless Son of God to be covered with all of our sins? What does that say about his love for us?

3. "Jesus took on the cross what you will have to take for all eternity *if* you don't take Jesus."

   a. Have you "taken" Jesus? Explain.

   b. Why do we sometimes think we can live for the sins that caused Jesus to have to die?

Put It into Practice

1. In the course of a few days, run your hands over several crosses whose owners permit such handling—churches, cemeteries, schools, etc. As you do so, try to imagine the physical toll that the cross took on Jesus.

2. Do you have a "besetting sin"? If so, what is it? What do you think it will take for you to get mastery over that sin? Pray that God would help you, by his Spirit.

50

His Grace, My Place

Turn Your Eyes upon Jesus

1. Read Matthew 27:15-26.

    a. Pilate no doubt had many prisoners at the time of Jesus's trial. Why do you suppose he chose Barabbas as a candidate for release (vv. 15-18)?

    b. What kind of emotional response do you suppose Pilate had when he received the message from his wife (v. 19)? Explain.

    c. Was the crowd's choice of Barabbas a spontaneous one (v. 20)? Explain.

    d. What question did Pilate ask the crowd in verse 22? How did the crowd respond? What follow-up question did Pilate ask (v. 23)? How did the crowd respond? Why didn't the people answer his questions?

    e. What was Pilate trying to do in verse 24? What kind of political move was this?

    f. What is chilling about the crowd's answer in verse 25?

    g. Why do you think Pilate had Jesus flogged before he sent him away to crucifixion (v. 26)?

2. Read Isaiah 53:10.

    a. Who put Jesus on the cross?

    b. What was the purpose of putting Jesus on the cross?

    c. What promise did God give Jesus, even as he hung on the cross?

Reflect on the Book

1. "The emphasis of the New Testament concerning Jesus Christ is not on his birth, nor his life, but on his death."

   a. Why does the New Testament focus on the death of Jesus rather than on his birth or life?

   b. How did some elements of Jesus's birth foreshadow his death?

2. "The cross was not primarily for *us*. The cross was primarily for God the Father."

   a. In what way was the cross primarily for God the Father?

   b. How does the cross most clearly and powerfully display the glory of God?

3. "The cross was all about three words: *mercy, justice, grace*."

   a. How was the cross about mercy?

   b. How was the cross about justice?

   c. How was the cross about grace?

Put It into Practice

1. Imagine that you knew you were born in order to die. How would you live your life differently? Ask a few friends the same question.

2. Do a brief study about the practice of crucifixion. How does this study increase your appreciation for what Jesus did for you? Thank him for his sacrifice.

51

The Warrior Rises

Turn Your Eyes upon Jesus

1. Read Mark 15:21-39.

   a. In your own words, describe the scene of the crucifixion (vv. 21-32). Who were the main characters, both good and bad? What did each of them do?

   b. What happened at the "sixth hour" (v. 33)? What was significant about this?

   c. Why did Jesus cry out what he did in verse 34? (See also Psalm 22:1.) How did some observers respond to Jesus's cry (vv. 35-36)?

   d. How did Jesus bring his life to an end (v. 37)?

   e. What happened to the curtain in the temple (v. 38)? Why is this significant?

   f. How did the Roman centurion respond to Jesus's cry and the way he died (v. 39)?

2. Read Romans 3:21-26.

   a. What "righteousness" does Paul have in mind in verse 21? How do the Law and the Prophets "bear witness" to it?

   b. How does someone acquire this righteousness (v. 22)?

   c. How is everyone equal in their spiritual deficits (v. 23)? How is everyone equal in their spiritual assets (v. 24)?

   d. Who did God present as a "sacrifice of atonement" (v. 25 NIV)? What is a sacrifice of atonement? How does this demonstrate God's justice?

  e. How can God be both just and the one who justifies
   every sinner who places his or her faith in Jesus (v. 26)?

Reflect on the Book

1. "That God allowed his own Son to be that warrior and lay
 down his life for humanity means that you are in a war you
 can't win."

  a. In what way are you in a war you can't win on your own?

  b. How does the death and resurrection of Jesus enable you
   to win the war?

2. "All of the wrath and punishment and judgment that your
 sin and my sin deserves, God put on this warrior who didn't
 come to kill, but who came to die."

  a. How can a God of love also be a God of wrath?

  b. Imagine you had been an eyewitness to the crucifixion
   of Jesus. To what element in that scene would you have
   paid special attention? Why?

3. "God doesn't grade on the curve but on the cross. And not
 just any cross, but the cross of the warrior who rises."

  a. What does it mean that God grades on the cross?

  b. At any time, Jesus could have chosen to come down from
   the cross (see Matthew 26:53). Why did he choose to
   stay on the cross and die?

Put It into Practice

1. Over the course of a week, seek out different artistic
 interpretations of Jesus hanging on the cross. What do you
 learn from these various works?

2. Take a day to repeatedly read and meditate on Psalm 22. Remember that Jesus had this psalm in mind as he hung on the
 cross.

Dead Man Walking

Turn Your Eyes upon Jesus

1. Read Luke 23:50–24:12.

   a. What happened to Jesus's body after his crucifixion (vv. 50-53)? Who took responsibility for this? Why did he do so?

   b. What did Jesus's female associates do after the crucifixion (vv. 55-56)?

   c. What did the women do immediately after the Sabbath ended (24:1)?

   d. What did they find when they arrived at the tomb (vv. 2-3)?

   e. What amazing encounter did they have at the tomb (vv. 4-7)?

   f. How did this experience jog their memories (v. 8)?

   g. What did the women do after this encounter (vv. 9-10)?

   h. How did the disciples respond to their report (v. 11)? Why did they respond in this way?

   i. What did Peter do in response? What did he think when he saw the scene at the tomb (v. 12)?

2. Read Hebrews 2:2-15.

   a. What question does the writer ask in verse 3? Why would he ask this question?

   b. How did God witness to the "salvation" he had provided (vv. 3-4)?

   c. What comparisons and contrasts does the writer make between Jesus and angels (vv. 5-9)?

d. Why did Jesus "taste death" (v. 9)?

e. Who is the "founder" of salvation (v. 10)? How did God make him "perfect" (v. 10)? What does this mean?

f. What does Jesus call us (vv. 11-12)? Does this make him feel embarrassed? Why or why not?

g. Why did Jesus share in our humanity, according to verse 14?

h. What did (and will) Jesus accomplish through his death (v. 15)?

Reflect on the Book

1. "Because Christ has faced and overcome death, he gives hope to all of us."

   a. How does Jesus Christ give you hope?

   b. Who do you know who needs the hope that Jesus offers? How can you help that person to find it?

2. "Everybody wants to know that they matter. We want to know that our life makes a difference here on earth and that somehow life continues after our journey on earth is over."

   a. In what way(s) do you want to know that your life matters? What would it take for you to believe that your life was worthwhile?

   b. What do you most anticipate about heaven? What are you most looking forward to experiencing?

3. "The presence of death does not mean the absence of God."

   a. Why does the presence of death sometimes make us think God is absent?

   b. Why would God call death "the last enemy" (see 1 Corinthians 15:26).

4. "We must answer Jesus's query to Martha: *Do you believe this?*"

   a. How do you answer Jesus's question to Martha? Explain.

Put It into Practice

1. It's often easier for us to *say* that we believe the gospel than it is for us to *live* it. Compile a list of all the pieces of evidence that could be amassed to indicate you are indeed a follower of Christ.

2. For one week, read the obituaries that appear in your local paper. What thoughts and feelings do you have after that week? How can you use those thoughts to motivate you to live out the gospel?

Other Harvest House Books
by James Merritt

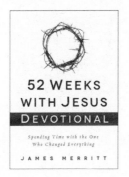

52 Weeks with Jesus Devotional

This year-long devotional (one entry per week) will reveal insights about Jesus and his ministry you may never have considered. You'll be inspired to embrace anew the Lord's invitation to "Come, follow me."

52 Weeks with Jesus for Kids

Do you long for your kids to fall in love with Jesus? Do you desire for them to understand what it means to really live for him? In an easy-to-read, kid-friendly style, James Merritt introduces kids (ages 9-12) to Jesus, explaining how much he loves them and demonstrating what it looks like to follow him. Each devotion includes engaging stories, scripture, a prayer, and a thought to consider.

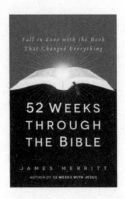

52 Weeks Through the Bible

For thousands of years, God's word has penetrated human hearts and transformed lives. So why does the Bible often collect dust on our shelves? Why don't we mine the wisdom filling its pages? Pastor James Merritt, author of the bestselling *52 Weeks with Jesus*, invites you to view Scripture afresh and fall in love with the book that changes everything.